Me, Myself, I

an anthology compiled by

Chas White and Christine Shepherd

Mary Glasgow Publications Ltd, London

This anthology © 1985 Chas White, Christine Shepherd
For copyright in the individual texts, see Acknowledgements and Index.

Design by Jack Tuckwood

Set in Novarese by Proset Photocomp Limited, Canterbury

Printed in Great Britain by Tisbury Printers, Salisbury

Published by Mary Glasgow Publications Limited,
140 Kensington Church Street, London W8 4BN

ISBN 0 86158 660 3

CONTENTS

1	**As small as the point of a pin**	Lennart Nilsson
1	**Copy**	Richard Armour
1	**Tears**	Kathleen
2	**The genius**	Frank O'Connor
3	**Saved from silence**	Martina Lenzi
4	**Family album**	Simone de Beauvoir
5	**Photograph**	Gareth Owen
5	**Looking back**	C. White
6	**Next best thing**	Joan M. Batchelor
6	**Watch this!**	Susan Clegg
7	**At Strachur**	Lorna Marshall
7	**My world**	Don Whillans
8	**Tara mam**	Brenda Leather
8	**Indian childhood**	Marion Ray
9	**The newspaper lady**	Christian Brindley
10	**No good crying now**	Valerie Avery
13	**Alice Dear**	Julie Teitelbaum
13	**Salford Road**	Gareth Owen
14	**My birthday treat**	Joan M. Batchelor
14	**Tadpoles**	Barry Hines
15	**Freedman**	Daniel Freedman
16	**Our dads**	Pupils of Notley High School
16	**Why?**	Thomas Grieves
17	**My dad, your dad**	Kit Wright
18	**The lesson**	Edward Lucie-Smith
18	**Going, going, it's here again!**	Colin Wells
18	**Dad**	Susanne James
18	**My papa's waltz**	Theodore Roethke
20	**The row**	Helen Moody
20	**Don't interrupt!**	Demetroulla Vassili
21	**Power drill**	Christopher Masters
21	**The wrong doing**	Marie Allum
22	**I don't think I'll ever get married**	Judy Blume
24	**The culprit of the vase**	Audrey Ryba
25	**The NSPCC**	NSPCC
26	**The Cruelty man**	Harry Weisbloom, *The Listener*
28	**What a brother!**	Sammy James

28	**My sister**	Steven Smith
29	**Terry**	Bernard Ashley
32	**Jealousy**	A woman from Southampton
32	**Angela**	Chris E. Shepherd
33	**That's me**	Julie Andrews
33	**Firecracker**	Marlene Fanta Shyer
35	**Nursing**	(advertisement)
36	**Lineage**	Margaret Walker
36	**Grandfather and I**	Paul Graham
36	**Grandfather**	Susan Hrynkow
37	**My gran**	Susan Boundy
37.	**My gramp**	Derek Stuart
37	**Yes, I can remember the coal mines**	Susan Springer
39	**The Lindens**	Lucy Clarke
40	**William's version**	Jan Mark
42	**Me and my family**	Kit Wright
43	**Rats!**	Philippa Pearce
44	**Keeping small mammals**	L. Firth (ed.)
45	**Heathcliffe**	(Anon.)
46	**Zeeta**	Denise Boyton
47	**Take one home for the kiddies**	Philip Larkin
47	**Nothing**	C. Marsh
48	**Cats**	A. S. J. Tessimond
48	**White cat in moonlight**	Douglas Gibson
49	**Tom-cat**	Don Marquis
50	**Ferret**	Keith Bosley
50	**How to catch newts**	John Walsh
51	**My newts**	Clarissa Hinsley
52	**A small dragon**	Brian Patten
52	**The turtles**	Tracey Clayton
52	**The lion**	Kevin Keenan
54	**That dumb old dog**	Judy Blume
57	**Unexpected charge of an enraged bull**	Betsy Byars
58	**Mortimer**	Joan Aiken
60	**Buying a pet**	Kim Archer
60	**Skeleton!**	Helen Moody
60	**Goldfish**	Alan Jackson

61	**I'm the hard one!**	John Gilbert
61	**Round one**	Ian Hardman
62	**Right!**	David Williams
62	**Nobody's putting me in no garbage can**	Betsy Byars
64	**Philip Hall likes me. I reckon maybe**	Bette Greene
67	**Too much water**	Gwen Grant
68	**Billy's game**	Bernard Ashley
70	**Monkey**	Leslie Thomas
71	**Signed: Your friend**	Jan Needle
72	**Edith**	Rosa Guy
74	**I'll tell your mum**	Jan Mark
75	**The hand**	Roderick Harris
76	**The worst kids in the world**	Barbara Robinson
76	**Anger**	Linda Rowe
77	**The cover**	Joan M. Batchelor
80	**Wedding bells: Greek style**	Angela Joannou
81	**The funeral dance**	Onuora Nzekwu
82	**Bonfire night and Mr Ellison**	Matt Simpson
83	**November 5th**	Sharon O'Sullivan
83	**Happy Christmas**	(Anon.)
84	**Albert and the liner**	Keith Waterhouse
87	**Breadcrumb's birthday**	Leslie Thomas
88	**The budgie's New Year message**	Kit Wright
88	**Dinner party blues**	Mick Gowar
89	**The weekly experience**	Karen Skeldon
89	**Look**	Michael Rosen
89	**Any Saturday in 1920**	Lil Smith
91	**Spare cash**	Her Majesty's Stationery Office
92	**Penny's home**	Prudence Andrew
92	**Horrible things**	Roy Fuller
93	**A removal from Terry Street**	Douglas Dunn
93	**Market day in Jamaica**	Suzanne Chantal Neita
94	**Ice on the Round Pond**	Paul Dehn
94	**I'm the big sleeper**	Michael Rosen
94	**The fight of the year**	Roger McGough
95	Acknowledgements	
96	Index	

As small as the point of a pin

Inside your mother's tummy there is a hollow organ called the womb. And you were inside that, in a 'bubble'. You were lying in a fluid which is very like water. It is called the amniotic fluid. While the baby is there, inside its mother, it is called a foetus and the 'bubble' is called the amnion. In the pictures you can see how the foetus lies in the amnion inside the womb. In the picture on the right the foetus is seven weeks old. It is turned sideways so you can see the head, arms and legs. The picture is made bigger and the foetus is larger than it would really be so that you can see it properly.

Very small foetuses can only be seen with a microscope which makes things seem a great deal bigger than they are.

When you were lying there, in the amniotic fluid, you floated around fairly freely. It didn't matter if you were upside down or right side up then. In the little picture at the top on the left you can see how funny you looked before you grew so big that your head and arms and legs could be seen clearly. At first you were as small as the point of a pin. Then you grew into something like a small crooked worm. When four weeks had passed your arms and legs began to show, but you had not grown fingers and toes yet. Already after seven weeks you started looking like a little baby, but your head was very big compared to your body.

Lennart Nilsson

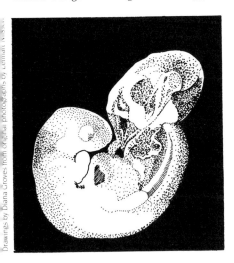

When you had been only four weeks in your mother's womb you looked like a little worm. You can see the head to the left; the round circle is the beginning of something that will become an eye.

This is the way you looked from behind when you were a six-week-old foetus. On top you see the neck because the head is bent forward. You can also clearly see what are going to be arms and legs.

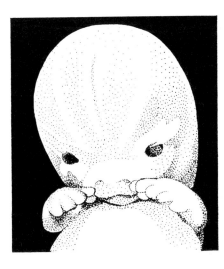

When you were seven weeks old you had eyes, nose and mouth. But your fingers were not very long yet.

Copy

His mother's eyes,
His father's chin,
His auntie's nose,
His uncle's grin,

His great-aunt's hair,
His grandma's ears,
His grandpa's mouth,
So it appears . . .

Poor little tot,
Well may he moan.
He hasn't much
To call his own.

Richard Armour

Tears

It began with a whimper,
The mouth became taut and drawn.
And then it opened as if to yawn.
And the eyes rolled wildly and stared forlorn,
The whole face wrinkled like a prune,
Its colour rose, and very soon
From deep within came a mighty yell,
A piercing scream with unchanging tone,
Pausing only for a mournful moan.
Bleary-eyed, unpacified,
The child had cried.

Kathleen

The genius

As I say, they squabbled endlessly about what I should be told. Father was for telling me nothing.

'But, Mick,' Mother would say earnestly, 'the child must learn.' 'He'll learn soon enough when he goes to school,' he snarled. 'Why do you be always at him, putting ideas into his head? Isn't he bad enough? I'd sooner the boy would grow up a bit natural.'

But either Mother didn't like children to be natural or she thought I was natural enough, as I was. Women, of course, don't object to geniuses half as much as men do. I suppose they find them a relief.

Now one of the things I wanted badly to know was where babies came from, but this was something that no one seemed to be able to explain to me. When I asked Mother she got upset and talked about birds and flowers, and I decided that if she had ever known she must have forgotten it and was ashamed to say so. Miss Cooney only smiled wistfully when I asked her and said, 'You'll know all about that soon enough child.'

'But, Miss Cooney,' I said with great dignity, 'I have to know now. It's for my work, you see.'

'Keep your innocence while you can, child,' she said in the same tone. 'Soon enough the world will rob you of it, and once 'tis gone 'tis gone for ever.'

But whatever the world wanted to rob me of, it was welcome to it from my point of view, if only I could get a few facts to work on. I appealed to Father and he told me that babies were dropped out of aeroplanes and if you caught one you could keep it. 'By parachute?' I asked, but he only looked pained and said, 'Oh, no, you don't want to begin by spoiling them.' Afterwards, Mother took me aside again and explained that he was only joking. I went quite dotty with rage and told him that one of these days he would go too far with his jokes.

All the same, it was a great worry to Mother. It wasn't every mother who had a genius for a son, and she dreaded that she might be wronging me. She suggested timidly to Father that he should tell me something about it and he danced with rage. I heard them because I was supposed to be playing upstairs at the time. He said she was going out of her mind, and that she was driving me out of my mind at the same time. She was very upset because she had considerable respect for his judgment.

At the same time when it was a matter of duty she could be very, very obstinate. It was a heavy responsibility, and she disliked it intensely – a deeply pious woman who never mentioned the subject at all to anybody if she could avoid it – but it had to be done. She took an awful long time over it – it was a summer day, and we were sitting on the bank of a stream in the Glen – but at last I managed to detach the fact that mummies had an engine in their tummies and daddies had a starting-handle that made it work, and once it started it went on until it made a baby. That certainly explained an awful lot of things I had not understood up to this – for instance, why fathers were necessary and why Mother had buffers on her chest while Father had none. It made her almost as interesting as a locomotive, and for days I went round deploring my own rotten luck that I wasn't a girl and couldn't have an engine and buffers of my own instead of a measly old starting-handle like Father.

Frank O'Connor

Saved from silence

I was born with a severe hearing loss. Some of my earliest memories are like Helen Keller's when she was a child.

It is awful to think that when I was a small child, I was like a bear! I gave my family a hard time. I was wild and was always demanding attention and every time I wanted something like biscuits, my mammy always made me say 'Biscuits' and when I said 'Biscuits', I always grabbed and ate them without saying thank you. Sometimes I was crafty enough to sneak in and get what I wanted instead of saying it first. I couldn't be bothered to say it and now I know that I was lazy. My family made me sit down and taught me to speak and gradually I found that I could talk like other people, but it took years.

I remember when a woman came up to my house to play toys with me. I know now she was a teacher of the deaf. Sometimes she showed me how to cook. When the woman took me away to the school, I felt strange because there were so many children there who were deaf or hard of hearing. I didn't like it at all and I cried to get back home.

Gradually, I began to like the school and the teachers did their best for me because they showed me how to control my tantrums. When I went home from school one day, I put my shoes away neatly in the corner and put on my slippers and put away my school-bag. This shocked mammy because I usually threw my things about in the house.

I can recall the day when I wore my hearing-aids for the first time. I hated them and I kept taking them off, but mammy made me wear them then and, gradually, I began to get used to my hearing-aids. I could hear with them, but without them I could not hear at all except for very loud noises like thumping sounds. After a while, I hated it without my hearing-aids because I could not even hear my mum's voice and, every time my hearing-aids were not working properly, I cried a lot until they were fixed.

Other memories I have are of going to the beach for the first time with my family. I loved playing in the sand and making pies out of it. I remember going into the sea with my daddy and I remember splashing the water over him. I couldn't even hear the swish of the waves or the laughter of the children who were playing. But I enjoyed myself thoroughly because my big brother and I collected sea shells and played games. [. . .]

My other brother, Peter, was a year younger than I was and he was awfully quiet. Every time my mammy put him in his cot, he just lay there and went to sleep. I was always the one that got mammy to myself all the time and Peter never really got mammy to himself because of me. I feel so ashamed when I remember this.

Today I am not like that because I am in an ordinary school where there is a unit for partially hearing girls and I know that I have been very lucky because I could have been sent to a boarding school. I am a fourth year student and will be doing my 'O' levels next year.

When I think over my early life, I realise how hard my family worked to give me speech and I am grateful to them because without their help, I would not be able to talk even today.

Martina Lenzi

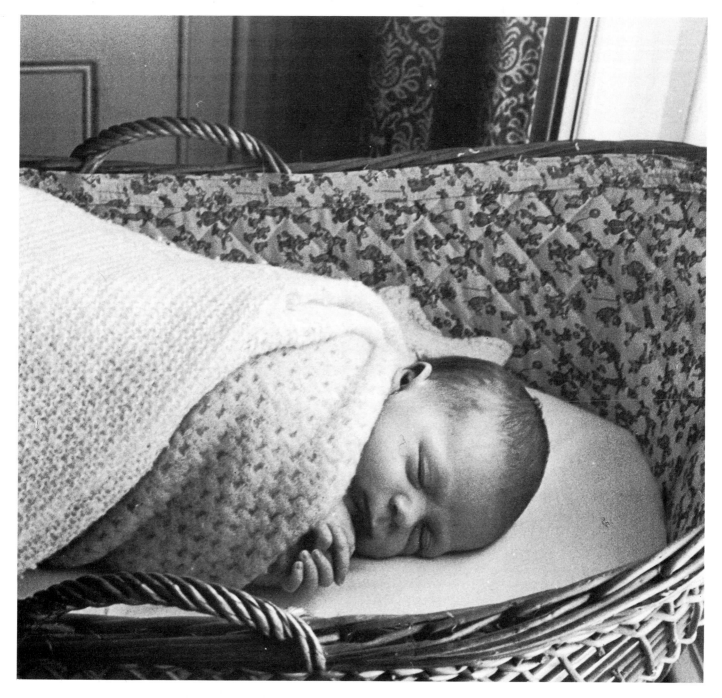

Family album

I was born at four o'clock in the morning on the 9th of January 1908 in a room fitted with white-enamelled furniture and overlooking the Boulevard Raspail. In the family photographs taken the following summer can be seen ladies in long dresses and ostrich-feather hats and gentlemen wearing boaters and panamas, all smiling at a baby: they are my parents, my grandfather, uncles, aunts; and the baby is me. My father was thirty, my mother twenty-one, and I was their first child. I turn the page: here is a photograph of Mama holding in her arms a baby who isn't me; I am wearing a pleated skirt and a tam-o'-shanter; I am two and a half, and my sister has just been born. I was, it appears, very jealous, but not for long. As far back as I can remember, I was always proud of being the elder, of being first. Disguised as Little Red Riding Hood and carrying a basket full of goodies, I felt myself to be much more interesting than an infant bundled up in a cradle. I had a little sister: that doll-like creature didn't have me.

Simone de Beauvoir

4

Photograph

Is that you and is that me
Captured by photography?
Is that Auntie, is that Dad?
Is that the face the face I had?

Are those clothes the clothes I wore?
Are those skies the skies I saw?
Those the hills that round me ranged?
Is it me or they have changed?

Did Auntie Gwladys wear that hat?
What made Beryl smile like that?
Why is Eileen staring right?
What was happening out of sight?

What the dreams that filled our heads?
What the words that once were said?
What would he I used to be
If he met me think of me?

Gareth Owen

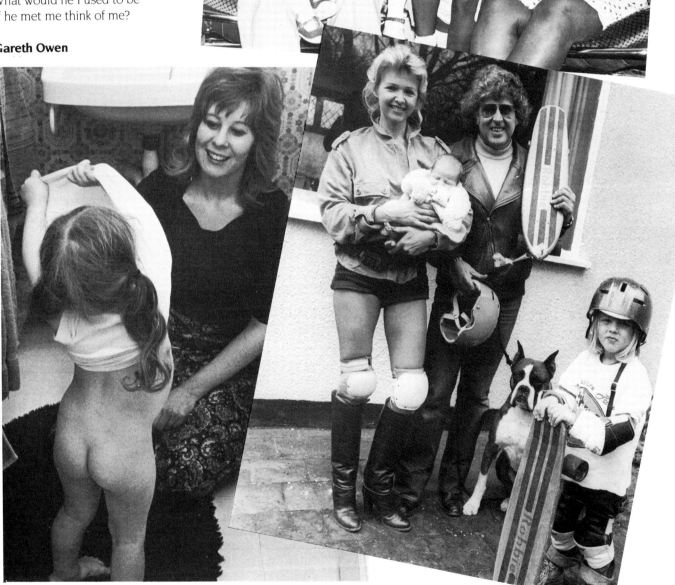

Looking back

Three years old, my face
Is frozen in an album.
Puzzled, shy and young.

C. White

5

Next best thing

Oh, I should have been a boy.
My dad wanted a son.
From the horse's mouth
I know, that he had ordered one.
Instead he got me . . . next best thing.
Bottoms out of knickers,
Toes out of shoes,
Socks tied up with ribbons,
So hair fell in my eyes
And mam making musical
The days, with her sighs.
Frillies, buttons and bows,
Handstands, races and dirt,
Tray-rides down the ashtip
Nails broken and knees hurt.

Oh little girl in boy's clothes,
Barefoot and free as air,
Little girl don't grow up
Stay bonny and brown and fair.
All the engine drivers,
And the engines then were steam,
Let you climb and stoke up . . .
Just hear the whistle scream.
Little girl, covered in oil and coal,
You should have been a son,
Yet you were the next best thing
When they ordered one.
But, how many tears did you cry?
How much anger did you feel?
How long did it really take
For time that hurt to heal?

Joan M. Batchelor

Watch this! ✓

When I was about six there were lots of boys and girls around my sister's age (about ten) who were playing a game of rounders in our street. Our road was a cul-de-sac, so all the children gathered around there.

It was a very energetic game which I was in the midst of. It came to my turn to bat. There was a boy called Vincent who always used to tease me and he called out, 'Watch this, she's so small she won't be able to hit it, she can't even hold the bat properly.' So I was determined to slog the ball. Vince bowled and I hit it. The boys gasped, the girls shouted and the ball went crash – straight into the window next door.

All the kids ran off and left me standing in the middle of an empty road, forlornly looking up at the shattered window. I felt drained of all feeling as I just stared up at what I had done. It wasn't my fault, I thought, it was that idiot Vincent who had made me do it, it was all his fault. I tried to convince myself, but deep down inside I knew it was really my fault.

John, our next-door neighbour, came down the stairs and opened the door. He looked unusually angry and this made me even more scared.

John was usually a nice man who gave me sweets, smiled a lot and told lots of jokes. But right now he wasn't smiling.

I looked up at him and gulped. Inside I was like jelly; I felt like falling to the ground. He turned and looked up at the damage. Then he turned and looked down at me.

Then he started to laugh. I couldn't believe it, he actually managed to laugh. I gave a weak smile, which was all that I could manage.

Susan Clegg

At Strachur

I was
Not much past three
It was raining at Strachur.
We were walking at Loch Fyne
I was wearing a raincoat.
It was pink with cats and dogs
Wearing sou'westers.
Soon the rain stopped
And I took off my coat.
It was still misty
I laid my coat in the sand
And forgot all about it.
Then the tide came in
And my coat sailed away
Like a small pink boat.

I remember fishing
Over a stone bridge at Strachur
With a jam jar on a string.
I kept the fish I caught
On the windowsill in my room
So they could see Loch Fyne
In the morning light.

Lorna Marshall

My world

My world was the backyard and the entry and a set of railings where the river flowed past and I could see the footbridge that crossed the river and was forbidden. My world was as far as I could see and as far as I was concerned anybody who went farther than that dropped off the end of the earth. [. . .]

My mother used to come and collect me from school. I remember thinking: 'I can make it home on my own.' So one day I tried it. I hung about for a bit, waiting for my mother, half hoping she wouldn't come but I knew she would so I went off early and wound my way through all these streets – my first bit of route finding – and I was really pleased and relieved when I got to the bridge and I could see the house.

I thought this was a really worthy effort because I couldn't think of anything bigger. My mother was very upset about it; she lectured and gave me a clout or two and I couldn't work this lot out at all. I thought it was a real big effort on my part.

We used to go in the river about five or six times a day. No towels, no trunks. I just sort of walked out of my depth and then I had to swim. I did some daft things there. I used to come out with my feet cut by broken bottles and there were hundreds of bloody black leeches that stuck on you. We used to have some good fun diving into great lumps of foam. 'Here's a big 'un', and we'd dive right in 'em.

One of the teachers told us that there used to be fish in the river and I couldn't see why there weren't any now. Then we found some and proved him wrong. Little tiddlers in some pools round an island. We used to explore down the river. There was a big log just off the bank and when the river was high it was covered. We played hours on that thing at 'King of the Castle'. Jumping on and off, scrapping, getting filthy and wet. You couldn't see the street from around the log and suddenly some kid'd shout, 'Hey, your mam's coming,' and there'd be panic, charging around after your shoes and socks. If my mother had found out that I swam in the Irwell she'd've killed me. Farther up the river there was a weir. That was a place that frightened hell out of me because there was a lot of water coming over and the river was wide at that point and you couldn't hear yourself speak. The water was churned up white and the kids said there were knives under it. I was scared stiff of the place. Later, there was one kid drowned there.

Don Whillans

Tara mam

Ta-ra mam.
Can you hear me? I'm going out to play.
I've got me playing-out clothes on
and me wellies.
What d'yer say?
Oh! I'm going to the cow-field.
I'm going with me mates.
Yes! I know tea's nearly ready.
I promise I won't be late.

Anyway, what we havin'?
Can't I have beans on toast?
What d'yer mean, mam, summat proper?
I ate me dinner (almost).
No, I won't go anywhere lonely,
and I'm going with Chris and Jackie,
so if anyone gets funny
we can all do our karate!

Yer what?
(Oh blimey. Here we go again.)
No, I won't go near the river.
I know we've had too much rain
and I won't go in the newsagent's
trying to nick the sweets.
Yer what, mam? I'm not. Honest.
I'm not trying to give yer cheek.

Wait mam.
Hang on a minute. Chris is here in the hall.
He says summat good's on the telly,
so I think I'll stay in after all!

Brenda Leather

Indian childhood

It was summer 1972, when I was four years old. At that time there had been many riots between students and police so we had invented a game suitably called 'Police and Students'. One group hid while the others chased them. Some of us were concealed in an orchard but we had to run and I was unable to keep up. There was a hole which the stray dogs had dug and as we stood there deciding what I should do, my bossy sister decided that it would make an ideal hiding place for me. Regardless of the surrounding sea of nettles, she picked me up jerkily and dumped me in the little hollow. I agreed excitedly when she told me that she would come and collect me later.

Unfortunately, I was, until now, totally uneducated in the evils of big sisters! I sat there presumptuously, extremely proud of not having been afraid of staying there alone. Not for long, however, because I suddenly heard a whine from somewhere behind me and something moved closer, growling. This was its territory and I was trespassing. Terror rose inside me. Within seconds I was encircled by about five stray dogs, one of which was the pack leader, commonly called Witch-Eyes for obvious reasons. They snarled and snapped their teeth trying to hint subtly that this was their realm. No matter how I tried, I could not extract myself from my precarious position among the nettles.

I had never been so terrified and it seemed like half an hour before my 'friends' came back. I discovered that they had finished the game ages ago and had come to collect me for lunch. They carelessly wiped away my tears and extricated me from the tangle of nettles. I'll never forget the malignant eyes of the dogs and my consternation as I looked at my palsied, stung limbs and then at the insensitive faces of my brother and sister.

Marion Ray

The newspaper lady

'Christian,' my father suddenly said as we were sitting round the Sunday breakfast table, 'you wouldn't like to get us the paper, would you?'

I thought. I felt that I really couldn't be bothered to, and thought of an excuse not to. 'I'm a bit too young, aren't I?'

'No. Six years old is enough to get the paper. We would be very grateful,' he said, in his forceful tone of voice. I knew I would have to get it in the end. 'All right. Where do I go?'

'To the newspaper lady on the corner.'

The words 'newspaper lady' suddenly shocked me as I thought of mutations of a woman with print and paper glued all over her face. I imagined a grotesque monster with huge rolling eyes and an enormous grey and white face. It was too late now. I had agreed to go, and that was it. My father gave me three ten pence pieces to buy the paper with, and told me to turn left out of the house and follow the pavement to the shop.

'Goodbye,' I muttered faintly. My parents looked strangely at me when I used that tone of voice, but my father said, 'Goodbye. Take care.' Take care. Did that mean that if I didn't, I'd be eaten up by the newspaper lady?

I left the room gingerly and went out of the front door, leaving it open behind me. I clutched tightly to the three coins in my hand as my hands started to sweat. Why had my parents put me into the danger of going to the newspaper lady? Didn't they want me?

Suddenly more pictures grew up in my mind of a woman with black hair, wet from ink, letters stamped all over her face, big black eyes and printing letters as teeth. I desperately wanted to go back, and I was just about to when a sudden thought struck me. If my parents had sent me to be killed by the newspaper woman, then surely that meant that they didn't want to see me again? If that was so, then they would probably have their own newspaper lady by now to eat me up if I came home.

I would get eaten up either way. I carried on down the pavement, and came to the corner. There was no cave or house or whatever the newspaper lady lived in. I stopped, wondering if I'd be able to see her or vice versa when I had turned round the corner. I told myself not to worry, and carried on.

From this point, I built up a resistance against the fear I had of the newspaper lady. I knew her face would be very strange, but I'd just laugh at it. After all, it would be an experience to see a face like hers. I built up a picture of her in my mind, the worst possible face I could imagine. She couldn't possibly have a face worse than this so I wouldn't be shocked or frightened. I felt it was quite an achievement. The sickly feeling in my stomach went as I felt my triumph over the newspaper lady. She would try to frighten me, but I would act perfectly normally and she would be beaten.

At last I got to the corner. There was an ordinary-looking sweet shop there. I went through the door confidently, and a bell jingled somewhere at the back of the shop. Behind the counter there was a doorway, going into a dark little room. That must be her room, I thought, and waited. Something started shuffling around in the dark room, muttering and growling as it did so. I tightened up and resisted the fear creeping up on me again.

'What d'yer want?' she said near the doorway of her cave, coming nearer to it. 'I'd like a . . .' She suddenly came out of the doorway. She looked like an ordinary woman! 'I . . .' My mouth fell open, and I dropped the coins and ran as fast as I could out of the shop.

Christian Brindley

No good crying now

I recalled that rainy Saturday when I was about eight. Mum
and I had to take my china doll, Jean, to be mended at a little
shop called the Dolls' Hospital, because my friend Jane had
dropped her on the pavement and her head had smashed
into a hundred pieces. I let out such a piercing scream that at
first Mum thought I'd been knocked over, and when I saw her
face as I held the broken doll in my arms, I wished I had been.
I wished it was my head that was broken.

In a mad frenzy she ordered me, Jane and Ida, my other friend
who was also crying, to search every square inch of the
pavement outside our house until every fragment was found.
Crying and crawling around on my knees, I picked up a
handful here and there, and we placed the tiny jagged pieces
on a tablecloth. Mum shouted at me that this was the last I'd
ever see of Jean again. She threatened to put her in the
dustbin and it would serve me right for allowing Jane to hold
her. Hadn't she warned me time and time again not to take
Jean out into the street? She was such a precious doll given
to me by my father when I was still a toddler, I was supposed
to play with her indoors and only upstairs in the front room
where there was a carpet, so that if I should drop her she
wouldn't break.

My friends scooted off to their houses for dinner, Mum tied
together the four corners of the tablecloth, then slapped my
legs so hard all the way up the stairs as I hugged Jean's
headless body, that I still felt the sting and could see the
imprints of her fingers for hours afterwards. We had waited
ages in the pouring rain for a 63 bus to take us to Peckham
before Mum decided we must walk there because the shop
closed for dinner between one o'clock and two. 'I reckon we're
going on a fool's errand anyway,' she kept saying as we
walked over the bridge. 'It looks to me as if it's broken beyond
repair. Perhaps this will teach you a lesson in future. I don't
say these things for nothing, you know. Jane makes sure she
doesn't bring any of her dolls out to play. It's always yours she
breaks, she sees to that. You are a silly little fool. And it's no
good crying now, you should have thought of all this before.'
[. . .]
In the small, dark shop various limbs hung from hooks
attached to lengths of string across the low ceiling. On
hearing the tinkling door bell these grisly arms and legs
began to dance, swaying independently as the little old man
emerged from somewhere at the back and caught them with
the top of his head. His abundant auburn hair might well
have been a wig since there wasn't a trace of grey, yet the rest
of him looked at least eighty.

He kept wigs of different colours, black, blond and auburn in
deep drawers under the wooden counter; some of them were
styled wavy like his, others were curly or straight. Inside
smaller drawers, glass eyeballs rattled and rolled about as he
tried his best to match them, but his own eyes didn't match,
for one was blue, the other brown and they stared blankly
without blinking for several moments, behind gold-framed
spectacles that magnified his odd-looking eyes.

He shook his head when he saw Jean. 'Oh dear! Oh dear!' His voice was high-pitched as though he had swallowed one of his doll's voice boxes. 'That's a very special doll, that is. I only keep a stock of average heads. I don't think I've got one big enough to fit, but I'll have a look.' Dolls' heads of different sizes, fair-skinned with rosy cheeks and dark-skinned, but all with strangely smiling faces waited on shelves all around the shop for their bodies to be fitted and limbs attached. He examined each likely head with Jean's body but kept shaking his auburn locks and tutting. 'No good! No good! The trouble is your doll isn't like the dolls I usually have brought to the Hospital.'

'Well,' explained Mum, 'she's not really a doll at all, you know, she used to model baby clothes in a shop window.'

I knew that Jean was no ordinary doll. She was real. She could talk, but only to me. She listened to every word I said, but only my words. She didn't like Mum and Gran when they were cross with me, in fact she didn't care for them at all. She thought they were both miserable and should have their heads boiled for making me cry. She only liked me and we had secrets that nobody else knew about, only Jane, but I wasn't sure about Jane, now this terrible accident had happened.

'I was wondering,' Mum continued, 'whether there was any possibility of your putting it together again. I know it's a lot to ask but you're so clever. I've brought all the bits and pieces along, that is, as many as we could find.' She delved down into her shopping bag and carefully placed the tablecloth tied in a bundle on top of the counter.

The man stroked his long auburn beard that might well have been doll's hair or perhaps he used his beard hair for all the bald-headed dolls that were brought to him.

'Well,' he shrilled, 'that depends on how many bits there are and how many bits are missing. It is a very big head and it's made from very special china. I've not come across one like this before.'

'They should all be here,' said Mum, untying the corners and helping to spread out all the pieces, triangles, squares and oblongs. 'Like a jigsaw puzzle, isn't it? I wouldn't know where to start.'

'Oh dear! Oh dear! It'll be a long job fixing all these pieces and I'll have to use some very special glue.'

'I don't mind how much it costs,' said Mum, looking at me ferociously. 'You'll have to go without your sweets and comics and we'll cut out going to the pictures on Saturday afternoons.'

'I'll do my best,' the man squeaked, sorting out the pieces and putting them into little piles, 'but it'll never be the same, you'll always see the cracks.'

'I don't mind,' I said, tearfully, 'so long as I can hold her. I don't mind what she looks like.'

'It's such a pity,' he shook his head. 'These dolls are so rare, so very rare indeed. Would be worth a lot of money. Victorian, I shouldn't wonder, but it won't be worth a light now, not now it's broken. What a pity! What a great pity! It really shouldn't have been played with.'

'Didn't I tell you?' Mum shouted, poking me in the ribs. 'I told you, didn't I? How many times have I told you not to play with her out in the street? Go on, you tell the doctor, you tell him.'

I burst into tears.

'No good crying now, is it?' she said, turning white with anger and sitting down on the wooden chair beside the counter. 'It's no good crying over spilt milk, is it? The damage is done. Just look at it. You should have thought of this when you defied me. I knew this would happen one day.' She turned to the man, who was examining each piece in turn as though it were a precious jewel, first closing one eye, then the other. 'I wouldn't have minded so much if she'd dropped it herself,' Mum went on, blowing her nose on a corner of the tablecloth. 'Give her her due, she's been ever so careful with it all these years. She's had it ever since she was three. Her father bought it for her. He got killed in the war, you know. That's what makes me so bloody wild,' she beat her fist on the counter, making the china pieces jump.

'When our house was blasted out,' Mum continued, 'you'd have expected the doll to have been smashed, but it wasn't. A miracle that was. To think that it survived all those war years, up and down the air-raid shelter, night after night, day after day – all through the bloody bombing because she wouldn't go down without her Jean. We were always the last ones down, but Annie, the lady who lived downstairs, always said that doll must have been a lucky mascot. We came very near to it with some of those damned doodlebugs. When you think it's been right through the blitz and it takes one of her bloody friends to drop it and do all that damage. It's really upset me,' her voice was breaking and she was screwing a corner of the tablecloth, nervously, 'I don't mind telling you. I keep seeing her father's face the day he brought it home for her. Pleased as punch he was and I told him off because I said it was too big for her to hold. I never thought then, that it would be the last we'd ever see of him . . .'

The man pushed his glasses to the top of his head and now it was clear that his eyes didn't match, neither did they move together. 'Such a shame,' he said. 'Such a great shame.'

'Soon after that, he went to fight in North Africa, then he ended up in Italy, fighting the battle of Monte Cassino. High up in those mountains, near a monastery – that's where he was wounded and left to die. We'll never really know what happened, will we? Some silly sod in the War Department sent the telegram to the wrong address; instead of it going to Trafalgar Avenue it went all round bloody Trafalgar Square. That's why I thought they might have made a mistake about the body as well. They sent me two different numbers for his grave, so I thought there might be a chance he was still alive. "Missing – presumed dead," it said. You remember the

telegram coming, don't you, Valerie? On your birthday.' Her voice was softer now and I nodded, watching the man deftly running his fingers over my wounded doll, imagining my father lying bleeding to death from great gashes in his body, being trampled on by other soldiers scrambling to safety among the craggy rocks and later on the vultures swooping down to peck at his carcase.

'I thought he might turn up one day. You live in hope, you refuse to believe – then came the brown paper parcel tied up with string. Inside were all his personal belongings – photographs of us, his wallet and letters I'd sent him that he never received marked "censored" and that awful word "deceased" – then I knew for certain there was no mistake.'

The man kept tutting and sighing. I didn't know whether he was expressing sorrow for my father or my doll.

'You understand why that doll means so much to me and her. He's buried in Bari in a war cemetery overlooking the Adriatic Sea – sounds a lovely place. I promised I'd take her there one day to see her father's cross, though I bet it'll take some finding, don't you? There must be thousands and thousands – I've got a photograph of it somewhere. When she's older I'll take her. The only trouble is I don't like the idea of flying and I'm not keen on the sea, so I don't know how we'll ever get there. I suppose we'll have to just wait and see. His comrades wrote me some lovely letters. One of them said he eventually died in a military hospital from deadly malaria, so I don't know what to think.'

I didn't know what to think, either. I was the only one in my class whose father had been killed in the war so I used to say he was still alive but he'd lost his memory in a monastery in Italy.
[. . .]

I was convinced that one day there would be a loud knocking on the street door, quite unlike anybody else's knock, and Gran would shout up the stairs in great excitement, 'Valerie! Valerie! Come down and see your father. He's returned home at last.' And there he'd be standing, looking very tall, dark and handsome in his soldier's uniform. He'd lift me up by the waist as high as the lamp-post and swing me round giddily; then he'd put his arms round Mum and kiss her. From then on she'd smile all the time, she wouldn't shout at me or smack me – we'd all live happily ever after.

'So what's your frank opinion about this doll?' Mum asked, standing up and folding the tablecloth now that the man had removed all the pieces and placed them carefully into heaps on a cardboard box.

He stroked his beard and squeaked, 'I'll do my best, madam. I can't make any promises, but I'll do what I can.'

'Well you can't be fairer than that,' said Mum, putting the tablecloth into her bag. 'Thank you for all your help. Say thank you to the man, Valerie.'

'Thank you,' I said.

'Leave it with me, and call back in a fortnight.'

Valerie Avery

Alice Dear

I had three dolls, Alice Dear, Patty and Judy. Alice had an all-rubber body and I could give her a bath every day. She had rooted hair and I could comb it and set it. When I spanked her, she always knew it was for her own good and that it hurt me more than it hurt her. She could take it like a lady. She didn't cry back at me like that old sissy Patty did.

Alice Dear was cuddly. She was just right in my arms. I could take her to bed with me and if she landed on the floor at night, she didn't mind at all because she knew I loved her. Patty would get mad at me, I know, because Mommy told me once that if she ever landed on the floor her head would break. I couldn't even consider taking Judy to bed with me. Her hard body always poked me and sometimes she'd get stubborn and stick up her leg.

Alice began to wear out from all the baths, and her rubber skin got all black. Though she never grew up like normal children, she got bald from all the times I washed and set her hair.

One hot July day of my ninth year, Alice Dear got a spanking for being naughty. Her soft body couldn't take it any more, and she split right up the back. All her foam rubber stuffing fell out.

I looked at her in surprise. Alice Dear didn't cry, she just gave up. All those shots in her behind from the times we played hospital together, she the patient, I the nurse, stood out like bruises. Suddenly I cried for all the times Alice never did.

I ran in the house and told Mother what happened and she comforted me. Then she took a paper bag and a broom and cleaned up Alice from the garage floor. She saved Alice's head. Alice Dear had a pretty face – rosy cheeks and blue eyes and a dimple that was nice to kiss. I set her head on the window-sill in my bedroom for a couple of weeks and then asked Mother about doll factories that take parts from broken dolls and make them into new dolls.

The next day, Daddy took Alice's head away. It was right about that time that I lost interest in dolls.

Julie Teitelbaum

Salford Road

Salford Road, Salford Road,
Is this the place where I was born,
With a green front gate, a red brick wall
And hydrangeas round the lawn.

Salford Road, Salford Road,
Is the road where we would play
Where the sky lay over the roof tops
Like a friend who's come to stay.

The Gardeners lived at fifty-five,
The Lunds with the willow tree,
Mr Pool with the flag and garden pond
And the Harndens at fifty-three.

There was riding bikes and laughing
Till we couldn't laugh any more,
And bilberries picked on the hillside
And picnics on the shore.

I lay in bed when I was four
As the sunlight turned to grey

And heard the train through my pillow
And the seagulls far away.

And I rose to look out of my window
For I knew that someone was there
And a man stood as sad as nevermore
And didn't see me there.

And when I stand in Salford Road
And think of the boy who was me
I feel that from one of the windows
Someone is looking at me.

My friends walked out one Summer day,
Walked singing down the lane,
My friends walked into a wood called Time
And never came out again.

We live in a land called Gone-Today
That's made of bricks and straw
But Salford Road runs through my head
To a land called Evermore.

Gareth Owen

My birthday treat

I was seven years old at the time,
Yet I remember it all so well.
In all my sleeping hours still,
I relive that fiery hell.

Mam woke me with excitement,
The Welsh love all bad news,
She thought it would be a treat for me
To give her fair dues.

'Would you like to see a fire
With engines and police too?
Grandad will watch the others,
I came back for you . . .'

The middle of the night it was,
Sleep stuck blurred my eyes,
A matter of a minute's walk,
Then feel excitement rise.

Many people stood watching,
Just like Guy Fawkes' Night,
I stood with mouth and eyes wide
At such a terrible sight.

Our sawmills, in full flame,
With crackles and 'Oh's' and 'Ah's',
Eyes like Roman spectators
While moving back their cars.

Then, to my utter terror
A voice shouted, 'Christ, the dogs!'
And I saw my dad disappear
Into the great, burning, crashing logs.

With the true Welsh sense of drama
The mumbling grew to prayers,
It was all right for the others,
It was my dad, not theirs.

I saw him for just a moment,
Black against the glare,
My heart stopped inside me
For he suddenly wasn't there.

'Dad!' I screamed, and met the eyes,
Heard the tuts of gleeful sympathy,
Such a lovely spectacle it gave
To see terror in such as me.

I felt my mam's arms about me
Then dad he stood right by,
He yelled, 'Why did you bring her, why?'
All I could do was cry.

I thought of all the horror,
As I still do each night,
Dad was safe next morning,
But my childhood died of fright . . .

Joan M. Batchelor

Tadpoles ✓

During a lesson on fact and fiction, Anderson is being asked to recall some facts about himself.

'What about when you were little? Everybody remembers something about when they were little. It doesn't have to be fantastic, just something that you've remembered.'

Anderson began to smile and looked up.

'There's summat. It's nowt though.'

'It must be if you remember it.'

'It's daft really.'

'Well tell us then, and let's all have a laugh.'

'Well it was once when I was a kid. I was at junior school, I think, or somewhere like that, and went down to Fowlers Pond, me and this other kid. Reggie Clay they called him, he didn't come to this school; he flitted and went away somewhere. Anyway it was Spring, tadpole time, and it's swarming with tadpoles down there in Spring. Edges of t'pond are all black with 'em, and me and this other kid started to catch 'em. It was easy, all you did, you just put your hands together and scooped a handful of water up and you'd got a handful of tadpoles. Anyway we were mucking about with 'em, picking 'em up and chucking 'em back and things, and we were on about taking some home, but we'd no jam jars. So this kid, Reggie, says, "Take thi wellingtons off and put some in there, they'll be all right 'til tha gets home." So I took 'em off and we put some water in 'em and then we started to put taddies in 'em. We kept ladling 'em in and I says to this kid, "Let's have a competition, thee have one welli' and I'll have t'other, and we'll see who can get most in!" So he started to fill one welli' and I started to fill t'other. We must have been at it hours, and they got thicker and thicker, until at t'end there was no water left in 'em, they were just jam-packed wi' taddies.

'You ought to have seen 'em, all black and shiny, right up to t'top. When we'd finished we kept dipping us fingers into 'em and whipping 'em up at each other, all shouting and excited like. Then this kid says to me, "I bet tha daren't put one on." And I says, "I bet tha daren't." So we said we'd put one on each. We wouldn't though, we kept reckoning to, then running away, so we tossed up and him who lost had to do it first. And I lost, oh, and you'd to take your socks off an' all. So I took my socks off, and I kept looking at this welli' full of taddies, and this kid kept saying, "Go on then, tha frightened, tha frightened." I was an' all. Anyway I shut my eyes and started to put my foot in. Oooo. It was just like putting your feet into live jelly. They were frozen. And when my foot went down, they all came over t'top of my wellington, and when I got my foot to t'bottom, I could feel 'em all squashing about between my toes.

'Anyway I'd done it, and I says to this kid, "Thee put thine on now." But he wouldn't, he was dead scared, so I put it on instead. I'd got used to it then, it was all right after a bit; it sent your legs all excited and tingling like. When I'd got 'em both on I started to walk up to this kid, waving my arms and making spook noises; and as I walked they all came squelching over t'tops again and ran down t'sides. This kid looked frightened to death, he kept looking down at my wellies so I tried to run at him and they all spurted up my legs. You ought to have seen him. He just screamed out and ran home roaring.

'It was a funny feeling though when he'd gone; all quiet, with nobody there, and up to t'knees in tadpoles.'

Barry Hines

Freedman

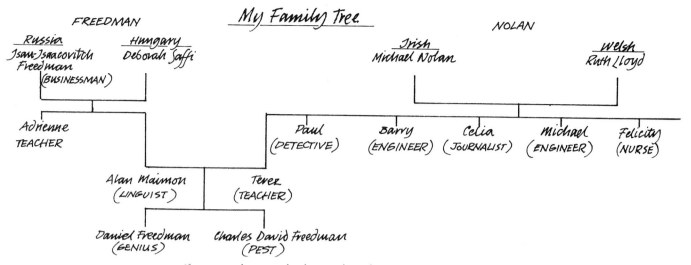

My Family Tree

FREEDMAN

Russia
Isau-Isaacovitch Freedman
(BUSINESSMAN) — Hungary
Deborah Saffi

NOLAN

Irish
Michael Nolan — Welsh
Ruth Lloyd

Adrienne
TEACHER

Paul
(DETECTIVE)

Barry
(ENGINEER)

Celia
(JOURNALIST)

Michael
(ENGINEER)

Felicity
(NURSE)

Alan Maimon
(LINGUIST) — Terez
(TEACHER)

Daniel Freedman
(GENIUS)

Charles David Freedman
(PEST)

If my grandparents had met when they were young, they wouldn't have understood each other! They each came from some far corner of the earth, and came to Britain in an odd way.

My mother's mother was the daughter of a Welsh sailor, who was shipwrecked off Southport and never returned to Wales.

My mother's father was of Irish descent; his own father had come to England because of the potato famine. My grandfather was brought up near Liverpool, where my mother was born.

On my father's side, my grandmother was from a remote part of the Austro-Hungarian Empire. Her family settled in Manchester, but she now lives in Brighton.

My grandfather came from Russia and was called Isau Isaacovitch (that was only his first name). He was Jewish, and after the Revolution he felt persecuted, so he emigrated to America. The border guard who had to fill in the immigration form could not spell Isau Isaacovitch, so he filled in the form like this:

Name **FREEDMAN, CHARLIE**

Age **UNKNOWN**

Nationality **RUSSIAN**

My grandpa was called Charlie from then on. When he moved to Britain he started a cloth business in George Street, Manchester. This is where my father was born.

When my mother was small, she lived in a very poor family. In contrast, my dad lived in a house with a chauffeur, maid and servants. During the war my dad escaped from numerous boarding schools, earning the name 'Houdini Freedman'.

My favourite relative is my Uncle Herbert, aged eighty, who is as thin as a rake and leaps around mending roofs. His spriteliness shows again in my grandma, whose exact age is dubious, but she has been telling us that she's seventy-nine for about a decade now.

Daniel Freedman

Our dads

There's one thing Dad doesn't like and that's someone who's got something he hasn't got such as a middle name. If I had had a middle name it would probably have been Djgashvili because my Dad likes Russian.

He's fairly strong and has a birthmark on his bum.

His hair looks like it's been sprayed with silver.

Anyone who's seen my dad with his shirt undone would notice his chest is particularly hairy.

He's always making corny jokes when my friends are at my house.

My dad makes me laugh when he wiggles his ears.

Most of the time we help him with the decorating and cleaning out the car.

He has big ears and wears flared Tesco jeans for work.

When my dad doesn't want us to know what he's talking about, he always speaks in Welsh. I now understand Welsh quite well.

Every night he goes to the pub after he has been to work.

His arms are long with large hands at the end.

When the tea's on the table he goes to the loo.

He takes size 11s mansize.

He can't swim because he won't let go from the side and he's frightened of getting his face wet.

Pupils of Notley High School

Why?

'Mum, why?'
'Oh, go see your father, dear.'
Clambering up 'knee-high' steps,
Clinging onto a handle, tugging,
The door opens onto the solitary ogre.

'Dad.'
'Yes Thomas?'
'How big is God?'
Silence, the newspaper lowers reluctantly.
A sigh.

The question repeated, a shrill whine.
'As big as a skyscraper.'
Harsh retort, the newspaper rises.
'Dad.'
Fingers twiddle.

'What's a sky raper?'
'Scraper! Skyscraper.'
I wait expectantly, innocently pensive.
'Well?'

'A very tall building, as high as the sky.'
'Oh.'
I leave, obediently closing the door.
Destination kitchen.
Target mummy.

Thomas Grieves

My dad, your dad

My dad's fatter than your dad,
Yes, my dad's fatter than yours:
If he eats any more he won't fit in the house,
He'll have to live out of doors.

Yes, but my dad's balder than your dad,
My dad's balder, OK?
He's only got two hairs left on his head
And both are turning grey.

Ah, but my dad's thicker than your dad,
My dad's thicker, all right,
He has to look at his watch to see
If it's noon or the middle of the night.

Yes, but my dad's more boring than your dad.
If he ever starts counting sheep
When he can't get to sleep at night, he finds
It's the sheep that go to sleep.

But my dad doesn't mind your dad.
Mine quite likes yours too.
I suppose they don't always think much of US!
That's true, I suppose, that's true.

Kit Wright

The lesson

'You father's gone,' my bald headmaster said.
His shiny dome and brown tobacco jar
Splintered at once in tears. It wasn't grief.
I cried for knowledge which was bitterer
Than any grief. For there and then I knew
That grief has uses – that a father dead
Could bind the bully's fist a week or two;
And then I cried for shame, then for relief.

I was a month past ten when I learnt this:
I still remember how the noise was stilled
In school-assembly when my grief came in.
Some goldfish in a bowl quietly sculled
Around their shining prison on its shelf.
They were indifferent. All the other eyes
Were turned towards me. Somewhere in myself
Pride, like a goldfish, flashed a sudden fin.

Edward Lucie-Smith

Going, going, it's here again!

Just as we go to bed, he calls.
We trot downstairs, cold inside.
We stand in a line in the dining room.
In front of a firing squad of questions.
Our dad, the Nazi General, his eyes
Blood red with spite.
'Who took the money?'
Butterflies start to flutter.
We looked at each other, silence!
Mum counts the money again and again.
It is denied by one, by two, by three.
The volcano erupts, boulders fly
. . . Silence!!!
'I've counted wrong, there is none gone.'
A sigh of relief as hearts stop pounding for another day.
The prisoners scatter.

Colin Wells

Dad

Gold-rimmed glasses
Glare.
Strong hands
Grip ferociously
A thin feeble shoulder.
The brown hairs on his scalp stiffen.
A hissing voice
That is bound in my heartshaped head.
'Why?'
The sound echoed,
Bouncing from wall to wall
Of my hidden cavern.
Hands loose,
Hairs relax.
Thin mouth . . . opens,
Reveals yellowed teeth.
Sound breaks out.
'Go to your room now!'
Spirit lags,
As do footsteps.
Door slams.
Size nine shoes stump away.

Susanne James

My papa's waltz

The whiskey on your breath
Could make a small boy dizzy;
But I hung on like death:
Such waltzing was not easy.

We romped until the pans
Slid from the kitchen shelf;
My mother's countenance
Could not unfrown itself.

The hand that held my wrist
Was battered on one knuckle;
At every step you missed
My right ear scraped a buckle.

You beat time on my head
With a palm caked hard by dirt,
Then waltzed me off to bed
Still clinging to your shirt.

Theodore Roethke

The row

It knew,
   that we were out walking!
It knew,
   that it would strike us
at the highest point of the Quantocks, it knew!
First the wind and then the rain
but then the hail had to go and stick his oar in
and aggravate them both.
That's what started it all.

Helen Moody

Don't interrupt!

Turn the television down!
None of your cheek!
Sit down!
Shut up!
Don't make a fool of yourself!
Respect your elders!
I can't put up with you anymore!
Go outside.
Don't walk so fast!
Don't run.
Don't forget to brush your teeth!
Don't forget to polish your shoes!
Don't slam the door!
Have manners!
Don't interrupt when I'm talking!
Put your hand over your mouth when you cough.
Don't talk with your mouth full!
Go to the market with me.
You spend too much money!
No more pocket money for you dear.
Go to your room!

Don't stuff yourself with sweets!
Don't point!
Don't go too near the television.
You are not coming out until you have tidied your room.
Don't interrupt when I'm talking!
Did you get any homework today?
Always carry a pen to school.
Eat your dinner up.
Wear your school uniform!
Turn the television over to watch 'Dallas'.
Bring any letters home from school.
Come straight home tomorrow.
Tidy your bed.
Don't shout!
Don't listen to my conversation.
Don't look at the sun it could blind you.
Don't bite your nails!
Don't suck your thumb!
Why don't you answer me!
You never listen to a word I say!
Don't interrupt when I'm talking!

Demetroulla Vassili

Power drill

Mum wanted a picture hung on the hallway wall. The wall is reinforced concrete and my Dad was drilling into it, when the strange incident happened.

My Dad had all his weight leaning against the drill, when it started to push out of the wall. Dad pushed with all his might, but it still reversed itself out of the wall.

It came completely out, so the bit was spinning in mid-air. The vibrations shook my Dad's hands so much he had to let go. It bumped down the stairs and turned. The drill headed for my foot. I pulled my foot away. Just in time too: the drill cut a groove in the toe of my shoe. My Dad and I went into the dining room and we told my Mum. She didn't believe us. 'Honestly, I never know what you two will dream up next!'

'But it's true . . .!'

'A power drill going mad,' said Mum. 'If I didn't know better, I'd say you two were stark raving bonkers.'

At that moment, the drill pushed open the door, chipping off the paint as it went. The drill vibrated forwards and set a groove in the skirting board.

It reversed out and at an angle to the settee, it moved along and scraped all the upholstery, sending bits of foam rubber flying everywhere. My Dad took it outside and poured water over it. My Mum put it back in the cupboard and we settled down to our evening meal. We were sitting chomping when Mum said, 'Listen!' A loud buzzing noise was heard from the cupboard. 'Oh no!' I said, 'Not again!'

Christopher Masters

The wrong doing

I spread jam on bread while listening
Mum starts again
Going on about Dad's moaning
I slump in a chair, staring at my untouched sandwich
A sick feeling rises from my stomach
Be quiet!
Dad regrets returning to England
Mum rejoices the day
I tap
Bored with the one-sided conversation
My choice is silence
Words would be against one
A voice calls.
Rising, leaving the forgotten sandwich
American football
The sound of heavy silence creeps through the gap under the
    door
My action was wrong.

Marie Allum

I don't think I'll ever get married

I don't think I'll ever get married. Why should I? All it does is make you miserable. Just look at Mrs Singer. Last year she was Miss Pace and everybody loved her. I said I'd absolutely die if I didn't get her for sixth grade. But I did – and what happened? She got married over the summer and now she's a witch!

Then there are my parents. They're always fighting. My father was late for dinner tonight and when he got home we were already at the table. Daddy said hello to me and Jeff. Then he turned to Mom. 'Couldn't you have waited?' he asked her. 'You knew I was coming home for dinner.'

'Why didn't you call to say you'd be late?' Mom asked.

'It's only twenty after six. I got hung up in traffic.'

'How was I supposed to know that?' Mom asked.

'Never mind!' My father sat down and helped himself to a slice of meat loaf and some Spanish rice. He took a few mouthfuls before he said, 'This rice is cold.'

'It was hot as six o'clock,' Mom told him.

Me and Jeff kept on eating without saying a word. You could feel what was going on between my parents. I wasn't hungry any more.

Then Daddy asked, 'Where's Amy?'

'In the den,' Mom said.

'Did she eat?'

Mom didn't answer.

'I said did she eat her supper?'

'Of course she did,' Mom snapped. 'What do you think I do – starve her when you're not around?'

My father pushed his plate away and called, 'Amy . . . Amy . . .'

Amy is six. When she doesn't like what we're having for dinner she eats a bowl of cereal instead. Then she races into the den to see her favourite TV show. But when Daddy called her she ran back to the kitchen. She gave him a kiss and said, 'Hi Daddy.'

'How's my girl?'

'Fine.'

'Sit down at the table and drink your milk,' he said
[. . .]

As Amy sat down she accidentally shook the table and her milk spilled all over the place. Mom jumped up to get the sponge.

'Don't be mad, Mommy. It was an accident,' Amy said.

'Who's mad?' my mother shouted. She mopped up the mess. Then she threw the sponge across the kitchen. It landed on the counter, next to the sink. 'Who's mad?' she hollered again as she ran out of the room and down the hall. I heard a door slam.

My mother's temper is getting worse. Last week she baked a cake. When she served it my father said, 'That's not mocha icing, is it?' And my mother told him, 'Yes, it is.' So Daddy said, 'You know I can't stand mocha. Why didn't you make chocolate?' And Mom said, 'Because I'm sick of chocolate, that's why!'

I love dessert and by then my mouth was really watering. I wished they would hurry and finish talking about it so I could start eating.

But my father said, 'I'll have to scrape off the icing.'

Mom looked right at Daddy and told him, 'Don't do me any favours!' Then she picked up that beautiful cake, held it high over her head and dropped it. It smashed at my father's feet. The plate broke into a million pieces and the chips flew all around. It was one of our ordinary kitchen plates. I'll bet if it was an antique, my mother never would have dropped it like that.

Later, when nobody was looking, I snitched a piece of cake off the floor. Even though it had fallen apart it was still delicious.

But that was last week. Tonight Mom didn't throw anything but the sponge. As she ran out of the kitchen my father cursed, crumpled up his napkin and got up from the table. Jeff pushed his chair away too, but my father hollered, 'You stay right where you are and finish your dinner!' He grabbed his coat and went out the back door. In a minute I heard the garage door open and the car start.

'You really picked a great time to dump your milk,' Jeff told Amy. He is fourteen and sometimes very moody.

'I didn't do it on purpose,' Amy said. 'You know it was an accident.'

'Well, I hope you're happy,' he told her. 'Because the whole rotten night's ruined for all of us now!' He cursed like my father and Amy started to cry.

'I'm going to my room,' she told us. 'Nobody loves me any more!'

Judy Blume

The culprit of the vase

I am fifteen and not long ago I had a difficult decision to make. My father turned up 'out of the blue' and pleaded with me to go to my grandmother's funeral. My mother was totally against it, but I had to go in spite of a painful memory.

I was about six at the time. It was like torture to awake each morning only to face my grandmother. She was strict, fussy and very tight-fisted. The house we lived in felt old, mainly because grandma filled it with all her 'ancient junk'. I thought it made the house seem very untidy. That was my reason for keeping friends away from it as much as possible. My grandma was very particular as well, only about little things though, like not touching her best china. The bedroom I slept in was plain and dull. There was a bare light bulb which protruded from the ceiling and the curtains drooped at the windows. I absolutely despised it.

My mind stretches far back to when my mother dressed me in all my newest clothes and smart fur coat. There was a feeling of excitement and happiness in me, though I could sense something was wrong; my mother was not coming with dad and me. When my dad attempted to explain, I remember the mixed up feelings inside me and the confusion. All I was told was that I would be staying at grandma's for a while. My dad stayed with me for almost a month, after which he left.

After that incident my grandmother was very bad-tempered. Jenny, at the time, was my best friend. She lived next door and she often invited me for tea. It was time for me to return the invitation.

'Grandma, please, please, please may Jenny come to tea?' I pleaded.

'Well,' grandma paused.

'Please,' I begged.

'As long as she behaves herself,' said grandma unenthusiastically.

The day arrived and Jenny crept into the lounge with me. Grandmother kept all her best china and pottery there.

Jenny wanted to see the large vase which stood on the mantelpiece. We were both very small, so I told Jenny she could take a chair and take the vase down. When Jenny had clasped it to her body she turned to give me the vase. It slipped from her and smashed to a thousand pieces. While I was doing my best to pick up the pieces, Jenny must have run out of the back door. I was so frightened tears came to my eyes. No sooner had my grandmother trundled in with her walking stick, than she said, 'Has Jenny not arrived? Well, maybe it is for the best.' Then she saw the broken pieces from the vase in my hands. At first grandma's face shook. I wanted to run away but something held me back. She raised her walking stick; I crouched down upon the floor. I tried to protect myself by throwing my arms around my body. I closed my eyes tightly. Grandma beat me and beat me. I thought she would never stop striking me with her oak walking stick. I screamed, 'Help, please! Help, someone!' The pain was indescribable. At that moment I became incontinent of my urine. I did not know when my grandmother had stopped.

The next thing I knew I was waking in hospital. There was a lady sat at my bedside. I could not believe it, my mother! She explained everything to me: about her divorcing my dad for committing adultery, her fight with the courts to take custody of me, and the real truth about my grandmother and the bad temper she could not control.

Audrey Ryba

The NSPCC

Where each £ came from

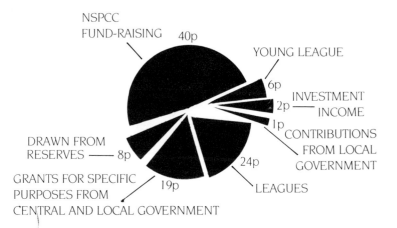

NSPCC FUND-RAISING 40p

YOUNG LEAGUE 6p

INVESTMENT INCOME 2p

CONTRIBUTIONS FROM LOCAL GOVERNMENT 1p

LEAGUES 24p

GRANTS FOR SPECIFIC PURPOSES FROM CENTRAL AND LOCAL GOVERNMENT 19p

DRAWN FROM RESERVES — 8p

How each £ was spent

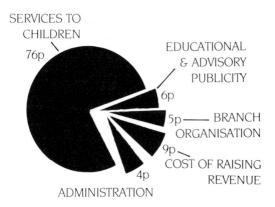

SERVICES TO CHILDREN 76p

EDUCATIONAL & ADVISORY PUBLICITY 6p

BRANCH ORGANISATION 5p

COST OF RAISING REVENUE 9p

ADMINISTRATION 4p

Casework Statistics

NEW CASES
15135 New cases
35474 Children involved

REFERRED BY
4554 Parent having charge
1862 Other relatives
5986 General public
2733 Official sources

AGES OF CHILDREN
13694 Under 5 years
20795 5 to 15 years
985 16 to 18 years

CLASSIFICATION
171 Accidental injuries
1307 Suspected non-accidental injuries
1676 Risk of physical injury
4134 One-parent family
2891 Cases of children left alone
3008 Neglect
2349 Marital problems
4346 Emotional problems
2503 Serious financial problems
1508 Housing problems

TREATMENT
665 None required – no case
6264 Closed or transferred
8206 Taken on for treatment

COURT ACTION
2 Adult prosecutions
133 Juvenile Court cases

OPEN CASES
4549 Carried over at the beginning of the year under review
11560 Children involved
4240 At the end of the year under review
10556 Children involved

VISITS AND INTERVIEWS
90617 Home visits
8703 Office interviews
6797 Case conferences
38532 Calls on other agencies
217 Enquiries for other groups
41800 Other casework visits.
3626 Student supervision sessions
1931 Group work sessions
2427 Meetings addressed on Society's work
1407 Fund raising events attended

GROUP WORK
14 Playgroups in England and Wales
316 Children registered
52 Playgroups in Northern Ireland
1008 Children registered
22 Mother and toddler groups
299 Children registered

SPECIAL UNIT REGISTERS
4055 Children on registers at the beginning of the year under review
3359 Children on registers at the end of the year under review
1452 Number of children added during twelve months
2148 Number of children taken off during twelve months

If you know, or suspect, that a child is being ill-treated or neglected, contact the NSPCC at once.

The Society also helps parents with problems affecting their children. All information is treated in the strictest confidence.

Don't keep it to yourself.

The Cruelty man

HOWARD Woolfenden has spent five years as 'the Cruelty' – one of the 250 inspectors of the National Society for the Prevention of Cruelty to Children. He is the acceptable face of social work on the daubed and window-smashed council estates, where families living on dole money can't afford the 80-pence bus rides to his office.

At 27, Howard has an uncompromising attitude to child-battering. 'Every parent has the potential, though obviously a lot of cases are the result of ignorance rather than overt cruelty. There are times when there is blatant, calculated cruelty to children, and that's when the public throws its arms up and says "Shock! Horror!" But there's a difference between that and the flash-in-the-pan injury at the end of a build-up of tension in the home. Somewhere there's going to be a trigger, something is going to prompt one or both parents to snap, and I can see quite clearly how that can result in injury.

'Certainly nowadays in Coventry we talk about finance, about housing, about unemployment, about poor marital relationships, difficult children. The child not being what the parent thought the child was going to be about; parenthood not being what the parents thought parenthood was going to be about. You get a combination of these things and sooner or later a parent is going to be pushed a little too far. It could be a baby crying at night, a child who won't do the washing-up when it's told, and somebody is going to snap, not necessarily because of what the child has done, but because of all the pressures on the family at that time.

'We do see very clearly that in some families a particular child is singled out. It can be the brothers or sisters who are the real irritation, but for some reason the other child is the scapegoat. This can be for many reasons. The mother may have had a bad relationship with her father and that child reminds her so much of her own father that she is going to pick on him. Or perhaps Dad has left home and the child reminds her of Dad, so that child is singled out for the treatment, the neglect, the rejection.'

Keith, a railway worker in his twenties, is one of Howard Woolfenden's 'flashpoint parents'. His attack on four-year-old Matthew is on the files as a 'non-accidental injury'. It happened when his wife Janice was out.

'I'd started work at five o'clock that morning and I didn't finish till five in the evening, and I lay on the settee with my head propped up on the arm, watching the television. Matthew was on the floor, just playing around. The next thing, I must have dropped off, and I could feel something on my face, like a powder. I opened my eyes, and realised that he'd emptied an ashtray on to me and all the ash was everywhere.

'I just didn't think. I just got straight off the settee and he went flying as I got up, and he bashed himself. I picked him up and shook him and I must have been holding him really tightly. I sort of dumped him on the settee, and when I looked round, the rent-book had been ripped and a £5 note in it had been ripped . . . and I just lashed out, I just went POW. Then I realised what I'd done, that I'd hurt him. I sat crying and then I put him into bed. I didn't say anything to Janice. I thought "What can I tell her? What do I say?" When Janice found Matthew badly bruised she took him to a doctor. The doctor contacted the NSPCC and Howard Woolfenden called on Janice and Keith. At first Keith wanted to know what business it was of an interfering busybody. But then, because there was somebody else there, because it wasn't just Janice and me, it helped to sort it out.'

Howard Woolfenden didn't even contemplate care proceedings. One way he has dealt with this family is to insist that Keith move out for a time, to force a breathing-space for the couple to work out their problems.

Taking children away from home and into care is very much a last resort for the NSPCC and for Howard. 'But I don't find it a particularly difficult decision to make. When I feel children shouldn't be at home any more, when the risks are too great, the bells are ringing loud and clear. We either make the decision on our own, because it has to be made there and then, or it's a team decision when we sit down with other agencies, the Social Services, the police, and discuss the children's future.

'When you go to take the children you can get varying responses. I remember one case where the children saw me and just scattered to all quarters of the neighbourhood. We had to spend quite some time rounding them up. But by night, when they were all settled, fed, clean and in bed, you could feel anxiety lifting from them.

I've also had children on the way to foster parents singing in the back of the car as they were on a trip, on a seaside outi. Although at the time it may seem like t last resort, we do see it as the first step getting things right, to having the childr return home again.'

And children do go home again. Thr year-old Donna Marie was the first o family of five boys and girls, all taken ir care after medical evidence of neglect, return home to her mother, Doreen. It w a drastically changed situation. 'Dore has matured through the experience, a the signs are looking good.' There was home help in attendance, plus visits fro a Social Services worker. Doreen was tending a family centre to help her pare craft. And Howard Woolfenden called, give support.

he NSPCC is one hundred years old , sadly, it is still needed. But there are ouraging signs. Nationally, a third of cases come from parents themselves ing for help, as well as from doctors, d teachers, and tip-offs from worried ghbours, some anonymous, but all ked into. Howard Woolfenden feels e is no longer a stigma attached to ing a visit from the NSPCC. 'It's not te the same as in years gone by, when pectors wore official uniforms and it an admission of failure to have us call. haps now we are seen more as a help- agency than just "the Cruelty".' What makes the NSPCC different from er caring agencies is its child focus. But can become blurred. Howard, married without children, took on his job 'be- se I love kids and I wanted to do some-

thing working with them and helping them. As it turned out, it's not quite what I expected, which was to be surrounded by kids every minute of the day. I spend a lot of time with the parents, because it's through them that, hopefully, I can help the kids.'

At the end of a week of crises, a shatter- ing blow for Howard. One of his cases that he felt had been successfully completed, with the family having worked through its problems, has to be re-opened. The mother comes to tell him that she is leaving home, that she does not want her husband to know until the day, and that she is sure Howard will pick up the pieces. For a start, he will have to tell her twelve-year-old son, who is in residential school during the week, that she does not want him home that weekend.

The meeting with the boy at school is surprisingly unemotional. The boy under- stands. His parents need a rest. He doesn't mind at all. But there is one small worry, 'My budgie – who will feed it? I won't let anyone else look after it.'

Tired, at the end of a punishing week, a moment like that can be devastating. But Howard Woolfenden says he has never thought of changing his job. 'I'm in the job for the kids, and whatever is happening with their parents or their home life, kids are generally resilient, they can take a lot and bounce back. That's what makes it all worthwhile for me.'

Harry Weisbloom, *The Listener*

What a brother!

My head throbbed with pain as I lay on my bed. I had been told to sleep but couldn't. My younger brother's mischievous little face popped around the door. I was on the verge of exploding already, without him there. 'Get us some corn-flakes, Sam,' his voice seemed to boom through my inner head.

'No!' I yelled. 'Get your own stuff, I'm sick of waiting on you hand and foot.

He was determined either to get his corn flakes or get me annoyed. He toddled in and plonked himself down on my bed. He then proceeded to jump about on it and meddle with the things on my dressing table. Whilst he was doing this he had a smug grin across his face.

His menacing ways were annoying me and the anger was welling up inside me – I was aggravated and he, I'm sure, was pleased to see it. I shouted at him but he wouldn't listen. I went over to him and grabbed him by the arm, he let out a scream but I continued to drag him over to my bed.

Once there I threw him onto the bed. I tried to turn him over, he was smaller than me so I managed to throw him onto his stomach quite easily. Then my hand banged down hard on his legs, with a crack like a whip. I was relieved of my anger. I saw a large red mark in the shape of my hand, printed upon his leg.

Adam started to cry, he ran out of my room and downstairs, sobbing as he went. Mum was in the kitchen – he told how I had hit him, but not how he had annoyed me. My Mum shouted, 'Come down here at once!' I slumped downstairs. 'What did you hit him for?' she asked.

'He was annoying me, Mum,' came my reply.

'Well I'm fed up with you hitting Adam,' she said. 'Now get upstairs and stay there.' Then she gave me a sharp slap, only managing to hit my arm; I ran into the hall and stamped upstairs.

I felt as if I hated my Mum. She wouldn't understand that he made me hit him through aggravating me. I went into my bedroom, slumped down on my bed and started to sulk. By now my head was really spinning. I was hot and sticky so I got into my pyjamas, lay on my bed and tried to relax.

Just then I heard my Dad coming up (probably he wanted to go to the toilet) and as I didn't want anyone to come in I slammed the door. He shouted at me, 'Stop slamming and banging, young lady.' So I got into bed and slowly dozed off.

It had all blown over in the morning, my headache had gone, so had the mark on my brother's leg.

Another NORMAL day loomed ahead.

Sammy James

My sister

'M-U-U-M, Steven . . .' my sister shouts down the stairs. 'Belt up,' I tell her, but once she has started, there's no stopping her. THUMP-THUMP-THUMP down the stairs into the living room. A few seconds, then I am summoned downstairs. A quick telling off, then, proud as a peacock she struts into the room. A horrible little smile on her face, laughter in her eyes, almost as if she's saying to herself: 'Ha, Ha, I've put one over on my brother.' But when she gets told off, boy does she hate it. She goes all miserable, sulks about the place and when she gets a real telling off, or she can't get her way, then she starts crying and screws her face up.

When she stops, her face is beetroot red, especially her eyes, and she sits there moping, or goes upstairs to play her recorder. That recorder! She comes in at night, eyes sparkling and flashing like killer rays, races upstairs and starts playing. It's the only thing that pleases her. Light of her life that recorder. Her brown eyes gleam and sparkle when she plays.

When she's quiet, it is luxury.

Steven Smith

Terry

'Sorry, Mum.'

It was the necessary form of words because the ticking off wouldn't be over until he'd used them. But he supposed it was a bit more than that, too. He really did feel sorry for her. She worked all day at the brush-works, and she rarely sat down in the evenings. She seemed more to collapse on the settee around about ten o'clock. She led a hard life and perhaps, as she said, they didn't always do as much to help her as they could.

'All right, never mind. Just try to be a bit more help from now on, eh?'

'Yes . . .' It was drawn out with a mixture of tolerance and resignation, a little bit grudging because it was so expected. But Mrs Harmer hadn't quite finished, and Terry knew what was coming next.

'Now, have you picked all the things up off your floor? If not, do it now, Terry - I want to hoover upstairs when I've cleared up this mess in the kitchen.'

'Yes . . .'

'Especially clothes and marbles . . .'

'Yes.'

'All right then.'

Mrs Harmer went back to her clearing up while Terry made for the stairs, reluctantly. The trouble with being kind and helpful at home was that it was so boring. Some kids he read about could be helpful by painting fences or chopping wood, or serving in a shop. All he ever got asked to do was pick up his clothes and 'be good'. You couldn't get more boring than that, he thought gloomily.

But he was in for a quick pick-me-up. As he got to the foot of the stairs his own full-length reflection in the hall mirror suddenly caught an approving eye. Oh yes! It really was a great shirt. He looked quite old in it, someone to be looked at twice. He stopped there and putting his head slightly to one side, winked slowly at himself, the performer and the audience in one.

'Can I just keep it on till tea-time, Mum? My shirt?'

Mrs Harmer was pouring milk into another saucepan and trying to kick the fridge door shut at the same time.

'Yes,' she called back, long-suffering. 'If you like . . .'

Terry puckered his lips at himself in the mirror, his head thrown back and his arms held wide for mass appreciation. The new discovery. Chart-buster. 'The Boy in the Black Shirt.' Frenzied applause and female screams of ecstasy filled his ears, and he waved to the cameras.

'You selfish little pig!'

Tracey had appeared at her bedroom door, her face twisted with disgust over the landing rail.

'Selfish little swank, you think you can get away with everything,' she spat at him. 'Mum, don't let him. Make him take it off.'

'Shut your mouth!' But Terry had learned long ago that you didn't shut Tracey up by standing and shouting at her. You took more direct action. He charged up the stairs with his head down, his feet drumming an angry tattoo on the tolerant treads. 'You shut up, Tracey! Keep your long nose out of it!' The swank bit had angered him, but her catching him posturing in front of the mirror had been worse; that was one of the biggest embarrassments of all.

Tracey stayed where she was long enough to see the strength of his reaction before diving for the shelter of her room. She knew that with her weight to the back of the door she could still withstand Terry's attacks, big as he was. But she just had time to yell, 'Mum! Mum! Tell Terry!'

Terry wasted no more words. He lunged for the top of the stairs and swung himself round the banister post on to the small landing in a practised movement which he'd perfected some years before in the long series of battles with Tracey. But she was no novice in that same theatre of war and her actions bore the hallmark of split-second timing. The door had slammed and Tracey had thrown herself against it before he made his furious assault.

'Chicken! Open the door! Let me in!'

'Mum!' came the muffled and breathless reply. 'Can you hear him?'

Mrs Harmer, who had certainly heard the thumping, the slamming and the shouts, was already on her way. In three or four angry strides she was at the foot of the stairs adding her own loud and unhappy comments to the commotion.

'You rotten kids!' she exploded. 'Can't you see I'm worn out enough as it is? All I ask is peace and quiet and a bit of doing what you're told. And all I get is this. Quarrel, quarrel, quarrel. Terry, come away from that door!'

She was half-way up the stairs, her head on a level with Terry's plimsolls through the bannisters. It was just impossible to grab his ankles through the railings: she knew, she had tried often enough before. He stood there, his back to the door, his face red and angry, his eyes filling with tears of frustration.

'Rotten Tracey!' he said, 'It's her fault. She won't bloomin' leave me alone . . .'

Mrs Harmer reached the landing and knocked authoritatively on Tracey's door, while Terry taking no chances, ducked his head in case the flailing hand was coming at him.

'Tracey, open this door. Come out here. I want a word with you.'

Mrs Harmer wiped the door with her sleeve where she had smeared it with the raspberry powder from an Instant Whip.

'Come on, hurry up.'

The door opened a cautious crack to reveal Tracey's pale but righteous face.

'Tell him Mum . . .'

'Come out here.'

'He's nothing but a rotten selfish pig. He thinks he can get away with anything, just because he's a boy. You used to be much more strict with me . . .'

Tracey stood back in her room, holding the door open, in a compromise position of safety both from Terry's foot and her mother's hand.

'Tracey, how many times have I told you not to cause trouble? We'd live a nice peaceful life if you'd just keep your remarks to yourself. Leave him alone. You're not his mother, I am. I'll deal with him if I have to. It's none of your business.'

'That's right,' said Terry, pleased to see his sister getting ticked off.

'And you!' Mrs Harmer suddenly turned and shouted at him, her patience completely exhausted. Her face showed all the strain of late nights, of trying to run a home and of doing a full-time job, as she returned to a familiar theme. 'All I ever ask of you children is that you behave yourselves and mind your own business and that's all you can ever not do . . .' She was too tired and fed up with them to put it any better. 'If you can't get on with one another, keep out of each other's way for God's sake! I've got enough on my plate without stupid quarrelling kids! And the sooner you two realize it the better.'

There was a moment's pause while Mrs Harmer's shouted remarks rang round the small landing, sinking in, before she shifted her weight ready to return to the milk downstairs. She sighed. Another crisis over.

But Tracey was unable to resist the temptation to have the last word. 'He gets away with murder,' she said in a low sulky voice as she began to shut her door.

'I do not!' Terry lunged at her but he was a slam too late and the hardboard panelling took the force of his battering hands.

'Stop it!' shrieked Mrs Harmer. She was really angry with them now, and frustrated at the situation suddenly getting out of control with so much to do and so little time before Jack came in.

'Spoilt little baby!'

'I'm not!' Terry deeply resented Tracey calling him a baby. She had always held her two years' seniority over him like some sort of debt he owed her.

'Yes you are, Mamma's little baby!'

'I'm not!'

'Where's 'our dummy, 'ickle baby?'

'Shut up!'

'Change 'is nappy, then?'

'You're asking for it!'

Mrs Harmer's shrieking voice reached a new high. 'Stop it! I said.'

'That's what you are! A little baby!'

'No I'm bloody not!'

That was the limit for Mrs Harmer. She whacked at Terry's head and caught him a stinging slap on the left ear. She was already furious and shaking as a result of the total disregard from the pair of them, and now she was both shocked and ashamed at hearing one of her own thoughtless swear-words coming back from the boy. Somehow she always imagined that he didn't hear what he wasn't supposed to. Perhaps it was because he had never copied them in her hearing before.

'How dare you? I'm not having that, Terry Harmer, not from a little boy like you.'

Tracey opened her door again, disappointed at having missed the climax. But the sight of Terry in tears and holding the side of his head told her all she wanted to know. A faint smile and a knowing look crept onto her face, an expression on tiptoe ready to vanish the moment her mother looked round at her.

'You've gone too far. I know I'll never go to heaven for what I sometimes say, but that's no reason for you to start using bad language. Tracey's right, I give you too much of your own way. You wore that shirt when I definitely told you not to, and now you start coming the old-soldier up here . . .'

Tracey's smile broadened and settled complacently on her face as she turned back into her room, her task of bringing Terry to book seemingly completed. She left the door wide open so that Terry would know that she was hearing it all while she brushed her hair at the dressing-table and hummed softly to herself.

Mrs Harmer went on, a bit more like a mother now instead of an angry woman. She was quickly calming down now that Terry had put her in control of the situation once more: and there was also the undoubted satisfaction of having clouted someone for the frustrations of the past five minutes.

'You're still my little boy, Terry Harmer, and while you're in my house you'll do as I say and you'll act decent. Now is that clear? Is it?'

She stood with her hands on her hips, leaning forward, her eyes boring into him. Terry, his head still ringing with the unlucky blow, and his eyes full with both the pain and the hurt of the injustice, felt his stomach suddenly leap over in angry rebellion. That's it! He pushed past his mother. He had had enough. To hell with the consequences. He didn't care any more. It was the sort of extreme mood he'd seen kids in at school when they'd shouted at a teacher. He thumped loudly down the stairs and snatched up his duffel bag from the bottom banister post.

'Terry!'

'I'm clearing off! No one wants me in this house. All you do is just shout at me and treat me like a baby . . .' He got to the front door, almost too choked to shout the words out. 'So I'm leaving. For good!' He threw the door shut behind him with all the force he could muster, clattering the letter-box and starting the wind-up bell ringing.

The slam shook through the house as slams always did, but tonight, being tonight, it carried through to the kitchen in just sufficient strength to stir the crockery in the sink. With a shifting, settling clatter the china pyramid collapsed, sending the milky saucepan bouncing off the rim of the sink to clang loudly across the kitchen floor, spreading a pool of dirty white water with it. For Gladys Harmer it almost drowned Terry's parting shot. But not quite. Anger and frustration had lent power to his vocal chords. He pushed open the letter-box flap and yelled at them both at the top of his voice.

'Bloody good-bye!'

Bernard Ashley

31

Jealousy

'I hated my sister's guts when she was born. When I say I was jealous, that's an understatement. I was six. I was staying with my grandmother, and they phoned to say that my mother had had a baby girl. Grandma said, "Aren't you lucky?" I said, "Tell them to send it back." And she smacked my legs for it. "God gave you a baby sister." But I hated her. I tipped her out of the pram, and when we had a bath together, I gave her soap to eat.

It's a wonder she survived. I can't exaggerate my feelings. I'm sure nobody had such a jealous childhood as mine. We couldn't be left in a room together for fear of what I might do to her. When she was five months old, my mother's sister, Auntie Jill, had a baby boy. We went to see the new baby, and jokingly, they said, "Shall we leave your sister for Auntie Jill and take the little boy home?" I thought they meant it. When it turned out they didn't, I screamed blue murder because we hadn't got rid of her . . .'

A woman from Southampton, quoted by Jeremy Seabrook

Angela ✓

For about two years, between when I was six and when I was eight, the thing I most wanted was to be an only child. I was sick and tired of our Angela – sick of seeing her, tired of hearing her and fed up to the back teeth of having to look after her and take her everywhere. She was really good at getting in the way and irritating me and my friends.

And to make it worse my mum had got it into her head that Angela was delicate. She was always telling people about it. It was just because Angela had had pneumonia and nearly died. So what! I'd had loads of things like chicken pox and measles. I didn't get so much as a bottle of Lucozade when I was ill. Angela had special foods for ages after the pneumonia had finished. My mum said it was to build her up. I think it had all been a bit overdone, myself.

It wasn't my fault she cut her head open but I seemed to get all the blame for it when the fuss had died down and the blood had been mopped up. I only pushed her because she'd pushed me. And how was I to know she'd fall over and hit her head on the corner of the fire grate?

We were both amazed by the blood. It spurted out like a fountain and even when Angela put her hand over the gash it found ways of shooting out. Except now it went in two or three different directions instead of just one.

Angela didn't cry or shout. She just sort of knelt there looking surprised. She didn't even seem to be in much pain. It was quite a few seconds before I realised I'd better go and get mum.

I went to the back door and shouted for her. She was in the garden hanging the washing out.

'Mum. Come quick! Our Angela's cut her head open.' Then I dashed back in. I thought I was quick but mum nearly got to the living room before me.

'Oh my God. I don't believe it.' Things had got worse since I'd gone to get mum. The cardinal red tiles were more or less swimming in Angela's blood and she'd started to cry, and was really sobbing and gulping.

'Go and get Aunty Dee. Go and get Mrs Worth.'

Now this appealed to me – a good dash to the neighbours on each side with the dramatic news.

But I didn't really see any more. I got shut out of the living room and had to listen out for details in the kitchen. I saw Mrs Worth fill and boil a kettle and then pour the water in a white pudding bowl and take it back in. I saw Aunty Dee rush home and come back with cotton wool and Dettol. (I bet our mum was too scared to remember where ours were.)

I heard Angela scream three or four times. I imagined her on mum's knee held tightly and rocked from side to side like a baby. I bet Aunty Dee was dabbing at the gash with disinfected water, and Mrs Worth would be holding the bowl.

The bowl stood for ages on the draining board after Mrs Worth brought it out of the living room. It was stone cold before the floating islands of cotton wool were taken out and squeezed, and the rusty red water was thrown down the sink.

My dad had to come home early and take Angela to the hospital. I just got ignored all afternoon. No one seemed interested in me, not even when it got to be tea time. It was only when Angela was in bed upstairs with four stitches in her head that anyone did take any notice of me. I don't know which was the worst – the lecture about being the oldest or the really hard smacks. It would just have served them right if they'd pushed me over and my head had got split open. But nothing good like that ever happens to me.

Chris E. Shepherd

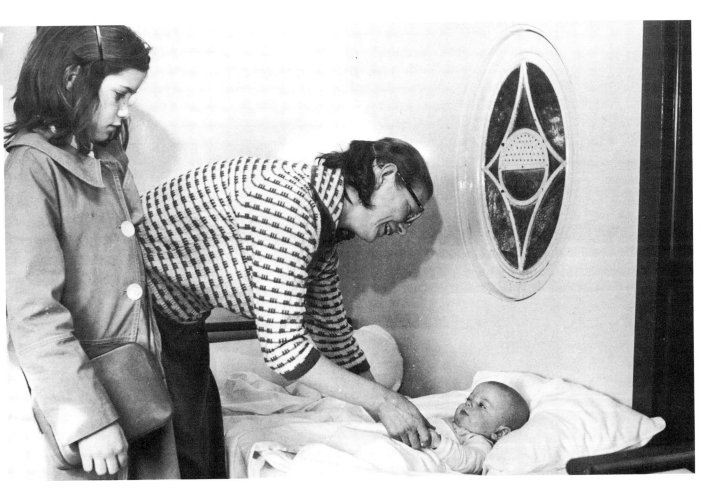

That's me ✓

Everything that happened that morning is so clear to me,
Although it was all three months ago.
'Will you be all right mum – you don't seem well?'
'Yes, off to school like a good girl.'
But I don't understand decimals this morning,
I don't want to change my library book,
   and yet I love reading.
Must I go to the swimming baths this afternoon?
Although I know I'm nearly ready for my green braid.
   I want to go *home*.
The four o'clock bell,
I race up the road until my breath heaves in my throat.

Near home I dawdle, linger, drag –
I can hear my own heart
   and my own footsteps.
A rush of speed up the path –
   a dash at the door –
Dad's smiling face meets me,
His laughing voice tells me I have a new brother.
'You're the eldest, you choose his name.'

The eldest! the big sister!
   That's ME.

Julie Andrews

Firecracker

Neil's parents have decided to care for his retarded thirteen-year-old sister at home. This is putting a strain on the whole family.

What happened was that for a long time my father couldn't get 'Firecracker in My Heart' written the way he wanted it. The refrain was great but the release never sounded right, and he said he could never concentrate enough to get good lyrics for the last eight bars with Gerri around. This time he wanted to make sure the song was recorded and the deal did not fall through, so very often after dinner he'd have to leave the apartment to go to his friend's house, where there was peace and quiet and no Geraldine.

One afternoon, when my mother was out and I was in my room, my father came home early. 'Anybody home?' he called the minute he opened the front door, and right away I could tell he was in a holiday mood. Gerri and I both came running immediately; the fourth of July sound in his voice meant something good was up.

'Hiya, Neil! Hiya, Gerri!' he said, and he practically zipped across the living room to the piano, pulled his 'Firecracker' music out of the bench and set it on the music stand, then plopped himself on the bench and loosened his tie. 'I think I really have it, Neil!' he said. 'Right in the middle of a phone call from Cincinnati when I was quoting the market price for IBM, it just flew into my head from nowhere. I better put it down quick before it gets away!'

My father doesn't get excited often, but he was really excited now. He opened the piano, tilted his head, and began to play. He played about three chords, then he stopped. He looked down at the keys, touched a couple of them and tried another chord. 'What the devil is all over these keys?' he asked.

I went over and looked at the keys. I touched a couple of them. 'They're sticky,' I said.

33

'What from? What are they sticky from?' my father said. The fourth of July went right out of his voice and the holiday expression disappeared from his face.

I figured apple sauce, but it didn't matter; we both knew they were sticky from Gerri, that it was Gerri who had messed up the piano, that it was Gerri, again and again, who was fouling things up, snafuing everything.

My father got up from the bench and stalked into the kitchen. I followed him; I guess I wanted to help clean up the keys so he could hurry and get started before he lost all the stuff that had come into his head during his phone call from Cincinnati. I rushed around and found a sponge, and he held it under the warm-water tap until it was soft enough to use, and I found the Ivory soap he told me to look for and then followed him back into the living room, and oh, good, grey grief, Gerri was sitting on the piano bench and just lifting a crayon to the 'Firecracker' music, pretending to write notes all over it like my father does.

My father flew to the piano and got there just in time to grab the crayon out of Gerri's hand, before she'd messed up the whole page. Then he threw the sponge on the floor and yelled at her.

Gerri started to scream and my father just stood there with his face turning redder and redder, holding on to the sheet music like it was a breathing baby and no kidding, his hand was shaking like there were no muscles or bones in it.

Finally, he pulled his eyebrows towards each other as if there was a stripe of horrible pain right behind them and he shook his head. 'I've lost it, Neil,' he said to me, and he made a fist with his hand and held it up to his mouth the way people do when they are trying to keep their hands warm. Then he slumped onto the piano bench and shook his head. 'It's gone,' he whispered.

Ten minutes later he was in the bedroom packing the suitcase he'd brought out of the storage room; it was the same suitcase we'd used to bring Gerri's stuff home from the training school.

Gerri was standing in the door of the bedroom, holding Woodie and watching. My father was opening drawers, pulling out socks and underwear and shirts, and stuffing them into the suitcase. His face was still red and his hands were still shaking.

'I've thought about this a long time, Neil,' he was saying. A long time. It's nothing sudden. The situation here – it's not good,' he said. I could see he was perspiring. His forehead was wet and a drop of wetness was moving down the side of his head in a straight line to his chin. 'As soon as I get . another apartment set up, I want you to think about coming to live with me. I think it's important for a boy of your age to have a peaceful home life without the sort of . . . pressures we're living under here.

'Dad, I don't mind,' I started to say, but even as I was saying it, Gerri had shuffled into the bedroom and begun opening dresser drawers and pulling out clothes and trying to stuff them into the open suitcase. I suppose I would have thought it was funny to see her pulling my mother's bras and pantyhose out of the drawers and think she was helping, but my father didn't think it was funny at all. I think he'd had

enough. He just threw a ball of socks on the bed like he hoped the socks would put a hole right through the mattress and he yelled, 'GERALDINE, STOP IT!' in a dragon voice that could shatter eardrums and must have travelled through three floors.

Geraldine's eyes opened wide and her mouth opened wider. She looked as if she'd peeked into a jack-in-the-box and a fiend had jumped out. Then, oh, good, grey grief, she wet her pants. I looked down at the rug where she was standing and saw this awful dark spot that was getting bigger and darker and right away I could see that my father hadn't missed it either.

He just walked out of the room and I heard him open the piano bench and clean out the music. He came back to stuff it all into his suitcase. Then he snapped the case shut and picked it up.

'I'm going to leave it up to you, Neil, I know you'll make a wise decision,' he said, and he went into the living room, wrote a short note to my mother, pushed in into an envelope, pasted it shut, and gave it to me to give to her. 'I'll call you soon,' he said and he set down the suitcase and put both his arms around me. Then he just held me and held me and I thought maybe he was thinking it over and changing his mind and would go right back in the bedroom and unpack and just stay here with us like always. Instead, he just gave me one more squeeze and ran his hand over his eyes, and then he picked up his suitcase and walked out of the apartment for good.

Without my saying a word, my mother could see something was wrong the minute she came home. She put down her packages so she could read the note my father had given me to give her, and she went over to the kitchen doorway and leaned against it when she opened the envelope.

Gerri had learned a new word, something that sounded like 'Womba,' which turned out to mean Mama. As soon as she saw Mum come in, she started saying, 'Womba, Womba,' because she was not only thrilled to see her mother come home but also seemed pleased with herself for improving her vocabulary. So while Mum read the note, Gerri kept yelling 'Womba, Womba, Womba' at the top of her lungs.

I said, 'Ssshh, Gerri, Shh,' really wishing I could stuff a couple of handkerchiefs in her mouth the way the crooks do on TV when they really want to shut somebody up, but I didn't want to upset my mother any more than she was already upset. So Gerri kept it up – *Womba, Womba* – sounding like a caveman about to throw a spear. I was watching my mother; her nose was getting red and she was pressing her lips together very tight. All of a sudden, she ran into the bathroom and shut the door; a minute later I heard water running. My heart felt like it was going *womba womba* too.

But she came out almost right away looking okay. She told me she wasn't really surprised that Dad had left. I told her exactly what had happened and she said she didn't blame my father, not one bit. Then she took Geraldine into the bathroom to clean her up and said that life was just going to have to go on and that we'd better start thinking about preparing dinner. She asked me to wash four baking potatoes and stick them in the oven. Then she quickly said, 'Not four baking potatoes, I mean *three* baking potatoes,' and she started to cry, and no kidding, it was awful.

Marlene Fanta Shyer

To understand the behaviour of a mentally handicapped person, you have to be constantly on the look out for tiny, but vital, clues.

Like spotting that there's one "to" too many in the headline below.

Take for example, Billy. Twenty one years old, with a mental age of 20 months, Billy is in no hurry to do anything.

He is entirely dependent on nurses to feed, wash, dress and take him to the toilet.

He can't speak and after three months' training, simple picture language still has him beaten.

The team that work with Billy are highly trained professionals. Nurses, doctors, psychologists and therapists.

They work very closely together, meeting regularly, often several times a week, exchanging notes, recording and plotting Billy's progress.

The dilemma they faced was the following:–

Was he incapable of communicating? Or was it that neither speech nor picture language were suitable communication methods for him?

One day, the nurse in the team, a Registered Nurse for the Mentally Handicapped (RNMH), was feeding Billy when she suddenly spotted that his right eye blinked rapidly when he ate.

Not the greatest medical discovery this century, you may think. But for Billy and the team, it was a breakthrough.

Further observation showed that Billy only blinked in this way at mealtimes. If he started to blink mid-morning or in the afternoon, it meant he was hungry.

Billy was communicating.

Immediately the team started work on a programme to teach Billy to communicate using signs and signals.

On the advice of the nurse, it was decided to control Billy's newest habit of waving his arms and legs in the air when he wanted attention.

Over several weeks, Billy was taught that by sticking one arm in the air he could catch the nurse's eye just as easily.

A small achievement and perhaps unnecessary? Small, certainly. But it served two main purposes.

First, when Billy started waving and kicking he wasn't misbehaving. He was bored. The programme gave him something to do. And because there was a reward (*or*

How observant have you got to be to to become a mental handicap nurse?

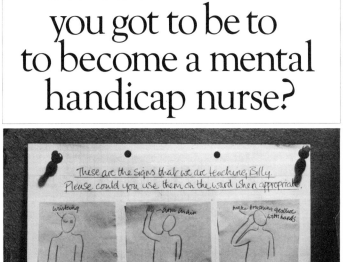

reinforcer) involved in the training, in the shape of a nurse giving him the attention he liked, he responded well.

But much more crucial, the programme demonstrated that Billy was capable of learning.

Billy could be taught.

Before long other signs were introduced into the training. These Billy picked up quickly. The chart pictured below, drawn by the psychologist on the team, was pinned up on the notice board in Billy's ward so other people could communicate with him.

It may look like childish doodles to you. But it represents the sum total of the team's progress with Billy over a twelve month period.

Now Billy is learning to use a spoon. This simple act has been broken down into 8 smaller stages. Each step is a separate challenge, like teaching Billy a new sign.

The process is painstakingly slow, testing the ingenuity, intelligence and patience of the nurse in a way no other job could do.

Nursing the mentally handicapped is not everyone's idea of a cushy number.

Certainly it's not for someone who thinks that nursing is only a matter of patting tops of heads and putting comforting arms round shoulders.

Although Billy is a long way off being able to live outside hospital and hold down a job, the objective of the team is to do everything they can to free him from total dependence on institutional care.

This is no pie-in-the-sky ideal. Most mentally handicapped people in this country live in the community.

It goes without saying that few jobs offer more of a challenge, demand more of your patience, give you more responsibility, or train you more professionally.

To qualify as an RNMH takes three years hospital and community experience, practical assessments and tough written exams.

During which time one of the biggest things you'll notice is the change in yourself.

For further information write to the Chief Nursing Officer, P.O. Box 702, (MH/96), London SW20 8SZ.

Nursing

Lineage

My grandmothers were strong.
They followed ploughs and bent to toil.
They moved through fields sowing seed,
They touched earth and grain grew.
They were full of sturdiness and singing.
My grandmothers were strong.

My grandmothers are full of memories.
Smelling of soap and onions and wet clay
With veins rolling roughly over quick hands
They have many clean words to say.
My grandmothers were strong.
Why am I not as they?

Margaret Walker

Grandfather and I

Piero is sharpening his sickle. I wish he wouldn't do it so early in the morning.

After a strong cup of Italian coffee, Grandfather and I went for a walk. The silvery-brown of the chestnut trees stood out against the blue sky. The ground was hot.

When we reached the shrine of San Rocco, I turned round to admire the village. I could see Uncle Freddie's home. His house is better than Grandfather's. He has a proper flush toilet.

I threw fifty lire into the enclosed shrine and walked on. We walked down to the river. Grandfather wouldn't let me drink any water until he had made sure there weren't any snakes about. He was very careful about snakes.

He whittled a stick. I watched. He looks like my aunt, I thought. Especially in the mouth and nose. We talked about Aunty Tranquilla.

'You must take a photograph of her before she dies. She is getting old you know,' Grandfather said.

He thought a lot about Aunty Tranquilla. I detested her. We decided to follow the stream onto some soggy ground. Swishing our sticks in the grass as we walked.

Grandfather said that he had killed five snakes near here when he was a boy. I felt uneasy.

It was about noon and the sun was hot on our necks. We climbed on up the stream while the humidity became worse. Blasts of cold air penetrated the damp patches on my shirt and the branches became more dense and twisted.

After easing our way through a patch of brambles, we arrived at an open spot. Grandfather was tired and he sat down.

Grandfather liked me. I was his only grandson. He was a small man, with fine thick hair. I am glad he has thick hair. They say that baldness is hereditary. That means that I won't be bald. He wears good quality clothes, but his trousers are too short and baggy. They flop about his ankles like pyjamas.

He stood up to empty the grass seeds from his turn-ups. There was a snake, black and shiny, about two feet away.

'Stay still,' said Grandfather quietly. Then with one careful blow he crushed its head with his stick. It was the first snake I had ever seen.

We carried on up the stream. I felt safe. I had Grandfather with me.

Paul Graham

Grandfather

I remember
His sparse white hair and lean face . . .
Creased eyes that twinkled when he laughed
And the sea-worn skin
Patterned to a latticework of lines.
I remember
His blue-veined, calloused hands,
Long gnarled fingers
Stretching out towards the fire –
Three fingers missing –
Yet he was able to make model yachts
And weave baskets.
Each bronzed Autumn
He would gather berries.
Each breathing Spring
His hands were filled with flowers.

I remember
Worshipping his fisherman's yarns,
Watching his absorbed expression
As he solved the daily crossword
With the slim cigarette, hand rolled,
Placed between his lips.
I remember
The snowdrops,
The impersonal hospital bed,
The reek of antiseptic.

I remember, too,
The weeping child
And wilting daffodils
Laid upon his grave.

Susan Hrynkow

My gran

I remember
Her curly, grey hair,
And her misty blue eyes
Deep set, in loosely wrinkled skin,
She was always knitting
Or busy in some other way.
Always bustling around
Never a moment's rest.
I remember
Her crooked fingers
And her broken finger-nails.
To remind her of her childhood
I used to listen to her intently
As she told tales of the war
And of her long-gone youth.
I remember
All of the china ornaments
She was so fond of
That now mean so much to me.
That nice way she used to laugh
It still haunts me.
I can hear it all the time
Ringing in my ears.
I remember too,
The dark musty church,
The reek of mingled perfumes
From crowds and crowds of people,
Many tear-stained cheeks
Of well-known faces
Yet none so well as
the memory of my gran's
Whose own ring
Was now resting on my finger,
And whose own uninteresting gravestone
Now stands right in front of me
Rapidly disappearing
Through a curtain of wet
mistiness.

Susan Boundy

My gramp

My gramp has got a medal.
On the front there is a runner.
On the back it says:
Senior Boys 100 yards
First William Green
I asked him about it,
But before he could reply
Gran said, 'Don't listen to his tales.
The only running he ever did
was after the girls.'
Gramp gave a chuckle
and went out the back
to get the tea.
As he shuffled down the passage
with his back bent,
I tried to imagine him,
legs flying, chest out,
breasting the tape.
But I couldn't.

Derek Stuart

Yes, I can remember the coal mines

One day as I sat to watch television the doorbell rang. It was my grandson. He was doing a project on old-fashioned coal mining. He said to me, 'Grandpa, do you remember the coal mines?'

'Yes,' I replied, 'I remember the coal mines.' My grandson looked at me with eager eyes so I went on.

'I remember getting up at four o'clock in the morning and creeping so I didn't wake your gran. I'd have a good breakfast and pack a lunch, then I'd set off.

'I would walk just over a mile to reach the mine and I was one of the "lucky" ones.

'Once there I would travel down the pit in the cage. Many pit faces were on average a mile from the shaft foot. Once down the pit I would walk one and a half miles to where I would dig. It was not an easy walk, most of it was a back-breaking and leg-tiring crouch.

'In some places the ceiling was so low that I had to crawl. I still have a scar on my back where I kept scraping it. Some men were daring and slid down the conveyor belt. I did that a couple of times but it hurt when I fell off so I gave up.

'When I reached the end of the dark tunnel with my Davy Lamp, I would kneel down, stripped to my shorts, sweating in the intense heat. If you think it's hard to dig standing up, you should try it kneeling. All the strain went on your biceps and tummy muscles. Even harder, you had to throw the coal over your shoulder.

'Our work was from six in the morning until eight at night. We took a quarter-hour lunch break in between. It was very stuffy. Air had to be pumped down. It was a relief to breathe fresh air and stand up when it was time to go home. Mining was very tiring, uncomfortable and hard. It took a lot of power, patience and muscle. I'm glad I'm finished.'

'That was a great story grandpa!' complimented my grandson.

'It was no story,' I said. 'Facts, all facts. I hope it helped.'

'It sure did,' said my grandson and he trotted off home.

Susan Springer

The family of Rev. Theophilus Woolmer (back row, second from right) and his wife Myra Field, née Oliver (seated with baby). Apart from a nurse (back row, left) and Myra's sister (back row, centre) all the others are children of Rev. and Mrs Woolmer, who were married in 1846.

A typical modern family.

The Lindens

One day when I was quite young, we went to see my father's parents at 'The Lindens' in Colchester. Grandad was a caretaker there, so that's where they lived. It was the office of the East Anglian Examining Board. Sometimes we went there for a day or two when it wasn't a working day. We had full run of the place. Grandad trusted us, he just told us not to muck about with anything. There were giant rooms, full of paper and packages and little Sellotape dispenser machines, clips, parcels, string. The smell of very fresh, clean paper and cold air hung about.
[. . .]

On that day Tony and I ran off to play a game and Grandad told us not to be long because we were going soon. After running around for a bit we decided to go to a particular room on the second floor. There was a little box-shaped open-faced lift there for putting packages in which were heavy and had to go downstairs. It was operated by two ropes at the side. Tony went downstairs and called up the lift shaft.

'Hello-ooo!'

I remember laughing and calling back. He said, 'Send the lift down, Lucy!' I did as he said. 'Okay,' he called back, 'Pull it back up!' I wondered what he was doing. I think I was a bit worried but it didn't seem we were doing something Grandad wouldn't like.

'Are you sure?' I called. 'What are you doing? Don't do anything silly.' I kept pulling on the rope. I got a shock as suddenly I saw Tony crouched in the wooden box, smiling at me. I knew he shouldn't have done it, I was frightened.

'Don't be silly,' he said, 'It's all right. Take me down again.' I was rather interested in this lift, it was fun – I felt a little adventurous so I did as I was told. When he was at the bottom again I told him to wait as I pulled the lift up again. I put my coat and slippers inside and sent them down. After playing about a bit Tony told me to get in. I couldn't! I was

scared. But Tony wouldn't take no for an answer, he was very persuasive so I got in.

'Be careful!' I called. 'A-are you s-sure?' The lift started to go down, I was in blackness and all I could see were the boards on the outside of the lift shaft. The open front made it more frightening – at least I could hear Tony's voice. I made it. Afterwards I felt I'd quite enjoyed it so I got him to send me back up again. As I was getting out at the top I heard a voice over the tannoy system.

'Tony and Lucy, wherever you are it's time to go! Hurry up, Grandad's getting impatient!'

Oh no, I had to hurry. The message came again. I called down to Tony. 'It's all right!' he said 'I'm coming up, go on pull! Just once more!' So I pulled as the message came again. 'All right, all right!' I shouted, 'We're coming!' I don't really know why I did that, there was no way that they'd be able to hear me. Just at that moment, Grandad walked in. 'I've been looking for you everywhere,' he said. I'd never known him to be angry before, that was the worst thing about it. I felt so guilty. I wouldn't think twice about it if it were anyone else but it was my lovely Grandfather angry with me.

'I-I-I've got to get Tony,' I stuttered. 'He's in here!'

'What?'

I could tell it was worse now, he knew we'd been playing with the lift. Frantically I pulled and pulled and almost fainted when I saw the empty box. That crowned it all. Tony always did go over the top, I could hear him sniggering from the bottom of the shaft.

But I was rather surprised, Tony got into worse trouble than I did; Grandad thought that Tony's little trick was the worst thing we'd done.

Lucy Clarke

William's version

William and Granny were left to entertain each other for an hour while William's mother went to the clinic.

'Sing to me,' said William.

'Granny's too old to sing,' said Granny.

'I'll sing to you, then,' said William. William only knew one song. He had forgotten the words and the tune, but he sang it several times, anyway.

'Shall we do something else now?' said Granny.

'Tell me a story,' said William. 'Tell me about the wolf.'

'Red Riding Hood?'

'No, not *that* wolf, the other wolf.'

'Peter and the wolf?' said Granny.

'Mummy's going to have a baby,' said William.

'I know,' said Granny.

William looked suspicious.

'How do you know?'

'Well . . . she told me. And it shows, doesn't it?'

'The lady down the road had a baby. It looks like a pig,' said William. He counted on his fingers. 'Three babies looks like three pigs.'

'Ah,' said Granny. 'Once upon a time there were three little pigs. Their names were –'

'They didn't have names,' said William.

'Yes they did. The first pig was called –'

'Pigs don't have names.'

'Some do. These pigs had names.'

'No they didn't.' William slid off Granny's lap and went to open the corner cupboard by the fireplace. Old magazines cascaded out as old magazines do when they have been flung into a cupboard and the door slammed shut. He rooted among them until he found a little book covered with brown paper, climbed into the cupboard, opened the book, closed it and climbed out again. 'They didn't have names,' he said.

'I didn't know you could read,' said Granny, properly impressed.

'C-A-T, wheelbarrow,' said William.

'Is that the book Mummy reads to you out of ?'

'It's my book,' said William.

40

'But it's the one Mummy reads?'

'If she says please,' said William.

'Well, that's Mummy's story, then. My pigs have names.'

'They're the wrong pigs.' William was not open to negotiation. 'I don't want them in this story.'

'Can't we have different pigs this time?'

'No. They won't know what to do.'

'Once upon a time,' said Granny, 'there were three little pigs who lived with their mother.'

'Their mother was dead,' said William.

'Oh, I'm sure she wasn't,' said Granny.

'She was dead. You make bacon out of dead pigs. She got eaten for breakfast and they threw the rind out for the birds.'

'So the three little pigs had to find homes for themselves.'

'No.' William consulted his book. 'They had to build little houses.'

'I'm just coming to that.'

'You said they had to *find* homes. They didn't *find* them.'

'The first little pig walked along for a bit until he met a man with a load of hay.'

'It was a lady.'

'A lady with a load of hay?'

'NO! It was a lady-pig. You said *he*.'

'I thought all the pigs were little boy-pigs,' said Granny.

'It says lady-pig here,' said William. 'It says the lady-pig went for a walk and met a man with a load of hay.'

'So the lady-pig,' said Granny, 'said to the man, "May I have some of that hay to build a house?" and the man said, "Yes." Is that right?'

'Yes,' said William. 'You know that baby?'

'What baby?'

'The one Mummy's going to have. Will that baby have shoes on when it comes out?'

'I don't think so,' said Granny.

'It will have cold feet,' said William.

'Oh no,' said Granny. 'Mummy will wrap it up in a soft shawl, all snug.'

'I don't *mind* if it has cold feet,' William explained. 'Go on about 'the lady-pig.'

'So the little lady-pig took the hay and built a little house. Soon the wolf came along and the wolf said –'

'You didn't tell where the wolf lived.'

'I don't know where the wolf lived.'

'15 Tennyson Avenue, next to the bomb-site,' said William.

'I bet it doesn't say that in the book,' said Granny, with spirit.

'Yes it does.'

'Let me see, then.'

William folded himself up with his back to Granny, and pushed the book up under his pullover.

'I don't think it says that in the book,' said Granny.

'It's in ever so small words,' said William.

'So the wolf said, "Little pig, little pig, let me come in," and the little pig answered, "No." So the wolf said, "Then I'll huff and I'll puff and I'll blow your house down," and he huffed and he puffed and he blew the house down, and the little pig ran away.'

'He ate the little pig,' said William.

'No, no,' said Granny. 'The little pig ran away.'

'He ate the little pig. He ate her in a sandwich.'

'All right, he ate the little pig in a sandwich. So the second little pig –'

'You didn't tell about the tricycle.'

'What about the tricycle?'

'The wolf got on his tricycle and went to the bread shop to buy some bread. To make the sandwich,' William explained, patiently.

'Oh well, the wolf got on his tricycle and went to the bread shop to buy some bread. And he went to the grocer's to buy some butter.' This innovation did not go down well.

'He already had some butter in the cupboard,' said William.

'So then the second little pig went for a walk and met a man with a load of wood, and the little pig said to the man, "May I have some of that wood to build a house?" and the man said, "Yes." '

'He didn't say please.'

' "Please may I have some of that wood to build a house?" '

'It was sticks.'

'Sticks *are* wood.'

William took out his book and turned the pages. 'That's right,' he said.

'Why don't you tell the story?' said Granny.

'I can't remember it,' said William.

'You could read it out of your book.'

'I've lost it,' said William, clutching his pullover. 'Look, do you know who this is?' He pulled a green angora scarf from under the sofa.

'No, who is it?' said Granny, glad of the diversion.

'This is Doctor Snake.' He made the scarf wriggle across the carpet.

'Why is he a doctor?'

'Because he is all furry,' said William. He wrapped the doctor round his neck and sat sucking the loose end. 'Go on about the wolf.'

'So the little pig built a house of sticks and along came the wolf – on his tricycle?'

'He came by bus. He didn't have any money for a ticket so he ate up the conductor.'

'That wasn't very nice of him,' said Granny.

'No,' said William. 'It wasn't *very* nice.'

'And the wolf said, "Little pig, little pig, let me come in," and the little pig said, "No," and the wolf said, "Then I'll huff and I'll puff and I'll blow your house down," so he huffed and he puffed and he blew the house down. And then what did he do?' Granny asked, cautiously.

William was silent.

'Did he eat the second little pig?'

'Yes.'

'How did he eat this little pig?' said Granny, prepared for more pig sandwiches or possibly pig on toast.

'With his mouth,' said William.

'Now the third little pig went for a walk and met a man with a load of bricks. And the little pig said, "*Please* may I have some of those bricks to build a house?" and the man said, "Yes." So the little pig took the bricks and built a house.'

'He built it on the bomb-site.'

'Next door to the wolf?' said Granny. 'That was very silly of him.'

'There wasn't anywhere else,' said William. 'All the roads were full up.'

'The wolf didn't have to come by bus or tricycle this time,

41

then, did he?' said Granny, grown cunning.

'Yes.' William took out the book and peered in, secretively. 'He was playing in the cemetery. He had to get another bus.'

'And did he eat the conductor this time?'

'No. A nice man gave him some money, so he bought a ticket.'

'I'm glad to hear it,' said Granny.

'He ate the nice man,' said William.

'So the wolf got off the bus and went up to the little pig's house, and he said, "Little pig, little pig, let me come in," and the little pig said, "No," and then the wolf said, "I'll huff and I'll puff and I'll blow your house down," and he huffed and he puffed and he huffed and he puffed but he couldn't blow the house down because it was made of bricks.'

'He couldn't blow it down,' said William, 'because it was stuck to the ground.'

'Well, anyway, the wolf got very cross then, and he climbed on the roof and shouted down the chimney, "I'm coming to get you!" but the little pig just laughed and put a big saucepan of water on the fire.'

'He put it on the gas stove.'

'He put it on the *fire*,' said Granny, speaking very rapidly, 'and the wolf fell down the chimney and into the pan of water and was boiled and the little pig ate him for supper.'

William threw himself full length on the carpet and screamed.

'He didn't! He didn't! He *didn't*! He didn't eat the wolf.

Granny picked him up, all stiff and kicking, and sat him on her lap.

'Did I get it wrong again, love? Don't cry. Tell me what really happened.'

William wept, and wiped his nose on Doctor Snake.

'The little pig put the saucepan on the gas stove and the wolf got down the chimney and put the little pig in the saucepan and boiled him. He had him for tea, with chips,' said William.

'Oh,' said Granny. 'I've got it all wrong, haven't I?' Can I see the book, then I shall know, next time.'

William took the book from under his pullover. Granny opened it and read, *First Aid for Beginners: a Practical Handbook*.

'I see,' said Granny, 'I don't think I can read this. I left my glasses at home. You tell Gran how it ends.'

William turned to the last page which showed a prostrate man with his leg in a splint; *compound fracture of the femur*.

'Then the wolf washed up and got on his tricycle and went to see his Granny, and his Granny opened the door and said, "Hello, William." '

'I thought it was the wolf.'

'It was. It was the wolf. His name was William Wolf,' said William.

'What a nice story,' said Granny. 'You tell it much better than I do.'

'I can see up your nose,' said William. 'It's all whiskery.'

Jan Mark

Me and my family

My mum is on a diet,
   My dad is on the booze,
My gran's out playing Bingo,
   But she was born to lose.

My brother's stripped his motorbike,
   Although it's bound to rain,
My sister's playing Elton John,
   Over and over again.

My baby sister's crying,
   She doesn't want her bath,
I have to stand there dancing,
   Trying to make her laugh.

What a dull old family,
   What a dreary lot,
Sometimes I think that I'm
   the only SUPERSTAR they've got!

Kit Wright

Rats!

Bill felt his way downstairs. He made for where the noise seemed to be coming from. He went from the foot of the stairs across to the kitchen. Much louder now: *Creak!* . . . *Creak!* . . . *Creak!* Clearer, too, the irregular sound of some kind of instrument that gnawed at metal.

And he became aware of a human undertone: a voice that whispered over and over again: 'Please, hush! . . . Please, hush! . . . Please! . . . Please! . . .'

'Sid,' said Bill Sparrow to himself, in wonder.

Across the kitchen to the walk-in larder. The larder door was only pulled to. Bill opened it gently, and shone his torch-beam inside.

Sid Parker crouched on the floor, in front of a cage in which two mouse-like creatures had frozen into stillness on the instant. One had been working a little treadmill fastened to the inside of a cage wall. The other had been gnawing at one of the bars of the cage.

'The creatures had frozen. But Sid himself turned his head slowly, to see who shone the torch. He said, 'They're gerbils. My gerbils. Mine.'

Bill said: 'Those things?'

'Yes.'

'They were making that noise?'

'Yes. They're not supposed to be up and about at night. But they are.'

'Like me.'

But Sid rarely smiled at his stepfather's jokes. He asked, 'Did Mum hear?'

'You bet.'

The kitchen lights blazed on; the larder door was flung wide; Alice Sparrow stood in the doorway, like a flaming torch, leaving no corner unlit, catching in her glare her husband and her son. Catching them red-handed.

'Well!'

The gerbils had flashed into life. One whisked out of his treadmill; the other from his wire bar. They vanished into the hay that stuffed the inner box of their bedroom. The only indication of their presence in the cage was the drumming of tiny feet on the floor of the bedroom. The gerbils were drumming the alarm for extreme danger.

Sid had covered his face with his hands.

As for Bill Sparrow, he dropped the jar of cold cream. It would have smashed and splattered on the larder floor, but his wife caught it, under her arm, as it began its fall. She was expert at preventing mess.

Then the row began.

Alice Sparrow made the row. Bill Sparrow sat on the bread bin, leaning against the larder wall to recover himself. Sid now stood up in front of the gerbils' cage, meeting his mother's gaze, enduring it.

'It's no use your trying to hide them! I saw them!' cried Mrs Sparrow. 'Rats!'

'No,' said Sid. 'Gerbils.'

'Don't you contradict me at three in the morning,' said Mrs Sparrow. 'They're smelly little rats. Where've they come from?'

'The toolshed.'

'And none of your cheek: *Where've they come from?*'

'A boy at school gave them to me. Jimmy Dean's cousin. He gave them to me with the cage, last week. I put them in the shed. But then the nights began getting colder. I had to bring them indoors just for the night. I had to. They're used to hot deserts.'

'They go back to Jimmy Dean's cousin tomorrow without fail. Today, that is. How many times have I got to say that we're not having animals in this house?. You've roller-skates and a camera and a transistor: what more do you want?'

'Two gerbils,' said Bill Sparrow in a mumble that no one heard.

Sid said: 'Mum, Jimmy Dean's cousin isn't at school any more. He's moved. Gone to Australia with his family. That's why he gave his animals away. So I can't give them back, Mum. Honest, I can't.'

She would not soften. 'Who gave them to Jimmy Dean's cousin, then?'

'No one. His dad bought them for him, in a Pet Department.'

She cackled with angry laughter. 'Some kids have fools for fathers. Where did you say he bought them?'

'The Pet Department in the Garden Centre.' Sid feared something – some plan – in his mother's mind. He was right.

She said: 'The Garden Centre isn't far. You can take those rats back.'

'They'll never take them back!' cried Sid.

'As a gift they will,' said his mother. 'They can sell them twice then, to two sets of fools.'

'Please, Mum!' He was almost crying.

'No! You take them back.'

'I won't!'

'Then I will. It'll make me late for work – and why I should have to carry a cageful of smelly rats! – But I'll take them.'

'Mum, they'll say they don't want any more gerbils, even as gifts. They'll have more than they can sell, anyway. Please, Mum, don't take them.'

'Rubbish!'

Bill Sparrow mumbled again. They paid no attention to him. Loudly, clearly, he repeated what he had said: 'I'll take them.'

Philippa Pearce

Keeping small mammals

What to keep

Some kinds of small mammals make good pets. You can learn a lot and have good fun keeping them. The kinds you could keep are white rats, white mice, hamsters, gerbils, guinea pigs and rabbits.

Remember that even the mammals that are easy to keep need to be looked after. Mammals are warm blooded, so they need regular meals. They also need to be cleaned out often. You have to do these jobs even when you are tired. You have to do them even when you want to do something else. You have to find someone to take care of your pets if you go on holiday.

Housing

Rats, mice, hamsters and gerbils are best kept indoors. Most guinea pigs and rabbits can be kept in outdoor hutches. They must be waterproof and have a warm sleeping compartment with a supply of bedding. If you are handy with tools you could make your own cages. Remember that all of these mammals can gnaw, so don't leave any bits of wood uncovered. You can buy plastic or metal cages for small animals. The bigger a cage the better it is. Gerbils could be kept in a fish tank with a metal lid. If you put sand in it they will burrow. Mice and hamsters like a cage with a wheel in it.

It is a good idea to put sawdust at the bottom of the cage. You can use paper for bedding or you can buy hay. Make sure the cage is ready before you bring your animal home.

How many to get

With any mammals, don't keep males and females together unless you want them to breed. Males can be fierce, so don't keep too many males together. Watch carefully when you put two strange animals together, you may have to stop them fighting. Mice are happy together and so are rats. Gerbils like company but hamsters are happier on their own. Guinea pigs like company. Rabbits can be kept on their own or together.

Feeding

Your pets should always have drinking water. You can buy a special bottle for them. Some small animals like to store food. Let them do this, but take away any mouldy food.

Cleaning out

This must be done every day. Take a good look at your animals and their droppings so that you can tell that they are well.

Breeding

Animal	Gestation[1] (approx. no. of days)	Weaned[2] at (days)	Litter size (approx.)
White mice	20	21	7
White rats	23	26	7
Gerbils	23	28	4
Hamsters	16	14	8
Guinea pigs	70	14	4
Rabbits	30	42	6

[1]Gestation – the time it takes for the young to develop inside the mother's body [2]Weaning – the time before the young can be taken from the mother.

L. Firth (ed.)

Heathcliffe

When he played with dad's new slippers,
We always forgave him.
When he devoured all the Sunday dinner steak,
We always forgave him.
When he christened the new lounge carpet,
Pulled feathers from the parrot's tail,
Locked himself in the coal cellar,
Rolled in the mud and then on the bed,
Decided to find out how long the loo-paper was,
Scratched the chair covers,
Tore the wallpaper from the wall,
Dug up the garden – and the dahlias,
 Made friends' with the postman,
We always forgave him.
But when he pulled at the tablecloth,
To see what was on the table,
Found out that our dinner
HAD been on the table,
It was too much!
We had to tell the Joneses,
To keep their dog,
Out of our house!

(Anon.)

Zeeta

Zeeta! What a name! But even so it fits her perfectly, and I've never heard another dog with the same name, so I feel proud really. Zeeta is my companion when I'm bored and she's also a constant source of entertainment. She's become a part of my life; it's become an automatic thing to pick up the lead in the morning and shout 'walkies'. That word! When she hears that she goes crazy. She jumps up and down, frantically wagging her tail and covering me with loving slobbery licks, her way of saying 'Thank you'.

Even now, at nearly twelve years old, Zeeta can run as fast, if not faster, than most dogs. She has a delightful habit of running away over the field and then bounding quickly back again, aiming straight for me and then swerving sharply at the last moment.

In appearance Zeeta looks like a stray. She has a scruffy coat and a constantly wagging, shaggy tail. Zeeta has a friendly but persistent nature. Once you've started stroking and fussing over her, she will not cease nudging you with a wet nose or

playful paw for more attention.

Zeeta is an exceedingly lovable character but she is very defiant (like me) and will stubbornly refuse to do what she's told. If she has done something wrong and she's sorry she hangs her head and gives me a sorrowful look.

Zeeta is a very fussy dog, particularly about her bed (an old pink blanket in a plastic basket). If she is not satisfied with it she will mooch about discontentedly and nose about in her bed until one of the family goes to rearrange it to her satisfaction.

Zeeta is an inquisitive character. If you were to give her a nut, for example, she would sniff it first, then if she found it quite harmless she would bite it to see if it was a treat. If it did not prove to be edible she would then roll on it. I gave her a piece of banana once – result: one exhausted dog with a very gungy, sticky, messy coat of hair. I'll never try that again.

Denise Boyton

Take one home for the kiddies

On shallow straw, in shadeless glass,
Huddled by empty bowls, they sleep:
No dark, no dam, no earth, no grass –
Mam, get us one of them to keep.

Living toys are something novel,
But it soon wears off somehow.
Fetch the shoebox, fetch the shovel –
Mam, we're playing funerals now.

Philip Larkin

Nothing

When I was young I always wanted a dog, a big dog that would protect me against my enemies. One day when I got home I could hear barking from the garden. It was my Uncle Tom's Alsatian. I heard my Uncle Tom say something about puppies.

I asked my dad if I was having a puppy for my birthday. He said I was not, which upset me.

I ran upstairs to my room and pushed my bed in front of the door to stop anybody getting in. I drew pictures of dogs thinking if I did have one I would set it on my Maths teacher who was my worst enemy.

On my birthday I was walking home from school when I heard a small dog yapping.

I ran into the garden and there was an Alsatian puppy. I was so overjoyed I ran up to the puppy and threw my arms around its neck and let it lick my face.

I tried to think of a name. 'Growler' I thought, but no, he was too playful to be called that. In the end I could not think of a name so I called him 'Nothing'. He answered quite well to it.

I started straight away to train him. 'Sit,' I said but he just went and weed up the rose bush. 'Roll over,' I said, he just looked at me. 'Kill,' I said, he came and licked my hand.

One day, after we had had Nothing a long time, he just did not want to do anything, he did not move, he just lay there. I went to stroke him. He snapped at me! All day he just lay there in the sun, not moving. The vet said that he had arthritis in his hind legs. I asked Mum what it was. She said it was nothing and Nothing would be all right, but he was not.

Every day he got worse and in the end he died while I was at school. I got home and went to him. I called him. No look around, not even a movement. He was dead.

C. Marsh

Cats

Cats, no less liquid than their shadows,
Offer no angles to the wind.
They slip, diminished, neat, through loopholes
Less than themselves; will not be pinned

To rules or routes for journeys; counter
Attack with non-resistance; twist
Enticing through the curving fingers
And leave an angered, empty fist.

They wait, obsequious as darkness,
Quick to retire, quick to return;
Admit no aims or ethics; flatter
With reservations; will not learn

To answer to their names; are seldom
Truly owned till shot and skinned.
Cats, no less liquid than their shadows,
Offer no angles to the wind.

A. S. J. Tessimond

White cat in moonlight

Through moonlight's milk
She slowly passes
As soft as silk
Between tall grasses.
I watch her go
So sleek and white,
As white as snow,
The moon so bright
I hardly know.
White moon, white fur,
Which is the light
And which is her.

Douglas Gibson

48

Tom-cat

At midnight in the alley
A tom-cat comes to wail,
And he chants the hate of a million years
As he swings his snaky tail.

Malevolent, bony, brindled,
Tiger and devil and bard,
His eyes are coals from the middle of Hell
And his heart is black and hard.

He twists and crouches and capers
And bares his curved sharp claws,
And he sings to the stars of the jungle nights,
Ere cities were, or laws.

Beast from a world primeval
He and his leaping clan,
When the blotched red moon leers over the roofs,
Give voice to their scorn of man.

He will lie on a rug tomorrow
And lick his silky fur,
And veil the brute in his yellow eyes
And play he's tame, and purr.

But at midnight in the alley
He will crouch again and wail,
And beat the time for his demon's song
With the swing of his demon's tail.

Don Marquis

How to catch newts

Over the hill and beyond,
There's a small secluded pond
With a slope of mud that's dried;
And there, to the sunlit side,
The newts come basking.
They're the wiliest newts for miles –
Slim three-inch crocodiles!
But you won't need Wellington boots,
Or a rod or a net; those newts
Are yours for the asking.

So you've never yet caught a newt?
Then I'll tell you the way to do it:
Crouch down by the water's edge,
And over the surface stretch
One arm, strong-handed;
Then the moment the water's clear –
(Newts near – but not *too* near) –
Swing your arm with a mighty splosh,
And up the smooth slope they'll wash,
Those newts, till they're stranded.
For a second their reptile eyes
Will goggle in small surprise;
Then, turning on flat spread feet,
They'll clumsily make retreat
To the pond's slimy bottom.
There are seven of them – take your pick!
Lift them up light and quick!
Into your jar they drop
One by one with a wet plop –
And hooray! you've got 'em!

John Walsh

Ferret

Ferret is a verb with teeth
for applying to pests. It
  stinks, has red eyes, sucks
blood. You must keep it muzzled

or it will become the verb
Kill and you will have lost it
  in the hole. Handle
with care what you cannot tame.

Keith Bosley

My newts

One night in thunder,
Two newts came to our back door to shelter
From the torrential rain and gusty wind;
I found them there when the rain had passed.

I caught them and kept them.
They are small and squirm when they are picked up.
Their stomachs and breasts are orange and black,
Pulsing with life.
They have four webbed feet and long shiny tails;
They are elegantly exact when they swim.

Out of the thunder night,
Came my black and orange dragons.

Clarissa Hinsley

A small dragon

I've found a small dragon in the woodshed.
Think it must have come from deep inside a forest
because it's damp and green and leaves
are still reflecting in its eyes.

I fed it on many things, tried grass,
roots of stars, hazel-nut and dandelion,
but it stared up at me as if to say, I need
foods you can't provide.

It made a nest among the coal,
not unlike a bird's but larger,
it is out of place here
and is quite silent.

If you believe in it I would come
hurrying to your house to let you share my wonder,
but I wanted instead to see
if you yourself will pass this way.

Brian Patten

The turtles

A paddling turtle in a pool,
Green waving weed below,
His aimless strokes stir ripples cool,
And bubbles rise and go.
With sudden gush and bubbling burst
Frothed water creams the brink,
Wide ripples spread their patterned wings,
I see the turtle sink
Through mists of grey-green watery tide
To join a friend on the other side.
They blink and laze with drowsy gaze,
One last limp stir, one shutting eye,
Then all is still where two stones lie.
Two patterned shells of turtlewood
Are dappled by the whispering weed.

Tracey Clayton

The lion

The small boy stared up at the large, tawny cat, which fixed one sleepy eye upon him. The boy sighed and stood, shifting from foot to foot. Gradually he plucked up enough courage to challenge it. 'Well, aren't you going to do something?' The lion didn't quite look as if it had heard.

'Don't just lie there; do something!' he blurted out but the lion just stared.

'Prowl around or gnash your teeth or something.' Still the lion stared.

'I don't think you are one.' He quickly stepped back, waiting to see what retaliation the lion would offer. But the lion blinked and stared.

'I don't think lions are fierce at all.' Still no response.

The child stood, not knowing what to do next. Suddenly he hurled himself at the bars of the cage and beat upon them with his tiny fists. The beast slowly rose to its full, magnificent height, and padded off to the far corner of its den. 'How fierce those human children are!'

Kevin Keenan

That dumb old dog

Sheila Tubman and her family are spending their summer in a friend's house in Tarrytown.

Jennifer is small with brown and white spots and long ears. When Libby saw her she cried, 'Oh, what an adorable dog!'

'She comes with the house,' Daddy said. 'She belongs to Professor Egran and she's ours for the summer.'

'I'm going back to the car,' I said.

Daddy held my arm. 'She can't hurt you.'

'Oh sure,' I said, pulling away from him. 'But I'll just wait in the car until you decide what to do with her. Because I'm not staying here if she does!' I ran down to the road, jumped into our car, and started to shake. How could they do this to me? Their own child. Their own younger daughter. Didn't they understand? Didn't they care?

Daddy and Mom hurried to the car. Mom stuck her head in the open window. 'Sheila,' she said, 'Jennifer is very small. She's more afraid of you than you are of her.'

'Did she tell you that?' I asked.

Daddy said, 'She's got a doghouse and a fenced-in area. She's chained up. You don't have to go near her.'

'Suppose she gets away?' I asked. 'Suppose her chain breaks?'

'That won't happen,' Daddy said. 'But even if it did, someone would catch her.'

'You're just saying that!' I told Daddy. 'But you don't mean it.'

'Have we ever lied to you?' Mom asked.

'Well . . . no.'

'Then trust us,' Daddy said.

I looked out of the car window. Libby was cuddling Jennifer. 'You promise she'll never come into the house?'

'I promise,' Daddy said. 'She's got everything she needs outside.'

'And you won't make me go near her?'

'Of course not,' Mom said. 'You can even pretend she's not there if you want.'

'And you won't make fun of me?'

'Do we ever may fun of you?' Daddy asked.

'Libby does,' I said.

'We'll see that she doesn't,' Mom promised.

'Now, don't you want to come into the house and see your very own bedroom?' Daddy asked.

'Well . . . I guess so,' I said getting out of the car.

We walked up the front lawn to the house. Libby was still holding Jennifer. When Jennifer saw me coming she jumped off Libby's lap. She barked and barked.

'You see!' I cried, turning around, ready to run back to the car. 'She hates me already!'

'Don't be silly,' Daddy said. He took my hand.

'I'm not being silly. Why else would she bark like that?'

'Because she doesn't know you,' Mom said, putting an arm around me.

'And she's never going to, either. I'll tell you that!'

We went into the house. The downstairs looked pretty nice, but I wanted to see my bedroom. So Daddy and I went upstairs while Libby and Mom poked around in the kitchen.

Daddy turned right at the top of the stairs and walked down the hall. 'Two of the bedrooms are this way and the other two are that way,' Daddy said, pointing. 'Since you wanted to be far away from Libby I thought you might like this one.' Daddy pushed open a door and smiled.

I went in. The first thing I saw was the dresser. It was piled with models of planes, boats, and cars. And the walls were full of team pennants. There wasn't even a bedspread on the bed. Just an ugly old grey blanket with CAMP KENABEC printed across it. I opened the closet door. The shelves were loaded with sports equipment. And where was my soft, fluffy, yellow rug with the big rose in the middle? No place. The floor was bare!

Daddy said, 'Well . . .'

'I hate it!' I shouted, running out of the room, past Daddy, and down the hall. I looked into the other bedrooms. But they were all the same.

'They're all boys' rooms!' I cried.

Daddy followed me and said, 'Well, of course they are. Professor Egran has three sons.'

When I heard that I got so mad I kicked a closet door and made a mark on it. Mom came upstairs then and said that wasn't a very nice thing to do in somebody else's house. Maybe it wasn't, but I didn't care.

Libby wasn't disappointed when she saw her bedroom. She doesn't mind having a boy's room. She loves it! She says it makes her feel very close to Professor Egran's fifteen-year-old son. Daddy says my room belongs to his twelve-year-old son. But if I hate it that much I can have the room which belongs to his three-year-old son, even though it's much smaller. I told him, 'No thank you. I'd rather sleep in a twelve-year-old's room than one that belongs to a baby.'

Mom said if we hurried and unpacked we could go for a ride round Tarrytown. So I went to my room and put my clothes away. When I opened the desk drawers I found six tubes of

Testor's glue, twenty-seven bottles of model paint, and a note. It said:

WARNING TO WHOEVER USES THIS ROOM
I HATE GIRLS! SO IF YOU ARE ONE LOOK
OUT! AND IF YOU TOUCH ANY OF MY
MODELS I WILL GET YOU SOME DAY!!!
B. E.

'Ha ha ha,' I said, ripping the note into tiny pieces.

After supper Daddy drove us around Tarrytown. It is a very hilly place. When you get up high you can look down and see the Hudson River. Of course you can also see it right in New York City. When I was younger I used to climb to the top of the jungle gym and look out at it. There is something about the Hudson River that makes you feel good, even if it is polluted.

When we came home I got ready for bed. Before I climbed in I looked out of my window. And what was right underneath my room? *Jennifer*. That dumb old dog! She looked up at me and barked. I barked right back at her. I knew we should have gone to Disneyland.

I got into bed. My room was very dark. I'm not used to sleeping all by myself in the dark. I closed my eyes but nothing happened. So I got out of bed and turned on the light. That was a little better. Soon the house was quiet. I knew everyone else was sound asleep. I tossed around for a while. Then I tried lying on my back. I looked up at the ceiling. I tried to think of something funny. Something that would give me a good dream.

That's when I saw the spider. He was running across my ceiling. I hate spiders! One time Peter Hatcher put a fake spider in my desk at school. When I took out my English book, there it was. But I knew it was a phony right away. So I held it by one leg and took it up to Mrs Haver. 'Just look what Peter Hatcher put inside my desk,' I said, shaking the spider.

Mrs Haver screamed so loud she scared the whole class. And Peter Hatcher had to stay after school for three days!

I looked at my ceiling again. The spider was still there and *this* one was no phony. 'Go away spider!' I whispered. 'Please go away and don't come back.' But the spider didn't move. He was right over my head. Suppose he falls on me, I thought. Suppose he's the poisonous kind and when he falls he bites me. Maybe I should put my head under the covers. Then if he falls on me it won't matter. No, that's no good either. He could crawl inside the covers and get me anyway. I could just picture Peter Hatcher telling the kids at school, *Did you hear about Sheila Tubman? She got bitten by a poisonous spider on her first night in Tarrytown. In twenty seconds she was dead!*

I jumped out of bed and ran down the hall to my parents' room. Daddy was snoring. I touched him on the shoulder. He sat right up in bed. 'What? What is it?' he asked.

'It's just me, Daddy,' I told him.

'Sheila . . . what do you want? It's the middle of the night.'

'I can't sleep, Daddy. There's a spider on my ceiling.'

Mom rolled over. She made a noise like *ummm*.

'Shush,' Daddy said. 'Go back to bed. I'll get it in the morning.'

'But, Daddy, he could fall on me. Maybe he's poisonous.'

'Oh . . . all right,' Daddy said, kicking off the covers.

We walked down the hall together. 'How did you notice a spider on your ceiling in the middle of the night?' Daddy asked.

'I have my light on.'

Daddy didn't ask why.

When we got to my room he said, 'Okay, where's your spider?'

At first I didn't see him. But then he started running across my ceiling. 'There he is!' I pointed. 'You see?'

Daddy picked up one of my shoes.

'Hurry,' I said.

Daddy stood on my bed, but when he smacked my shoe against the ceiling the spider ran the other way.

I tried to help. I gave him directions. 'That's it,' I called. 'Now just a little to the left. No, no, now to the right. Hit him, Daddy! Hit him now!'

But Daddy missed him every time. He was running up and down my bed, but the spider ran faster.

Just as Daddy said, 'I give up,' he got him. Squish . . . that was the end of my spider. There was a big black mark on the ceiling. But I felt a whole lot better.

'Now, would you please go back to sleep!' Daddy said.

'I'll try.'

'And if you find anything else unusual . . . tell me about it in the morning.'

'Okay,' I said, snuggling under the covers.

I think I fell asleep then. But a few hours later I woke up. I heard this really scary noise. It sounded like *whooo whooo whooo*. I didn't know what to do. I buried my head under the pillow, but that didn't help. I could still hear it. I thought about what it might be – a ghost, or a vampire, or even an ordinary monster.

I got up and ran back down the hall. Daddy was snoring much louder now. This time I walked around to Mom's side of the bed and shook her a little. She jumped up.

'Oh, Sheila!' she said, when she saw who it was. 'You scared me!'

'I'm sorry,' I whispered.

'What is it?'

'It's a noise in my room,' I said.

'Go back to sleep,' Mom told me. 'It's nothing.'

'How do you know?' I asked. 'You haven't heard it. It sounds like a ghost.'

'There aren't any ghosts!'

'Please, Mom, please come and see.'

'Oh . . . all right.' She put on her robe and we went down the hall to my room. 'Well,' Mom said, 'Where's your noise?'

'Just wait,' I told her.

56

She sat down on my bed and yawned. Soon it started again. *Whooo . . . whooo . . .*

'You see?' I said, throwing my arms around Mom. I could tell from her face that she didn't like the noise either. 'You want me to go wake Daddy?' I asked.

'No, not yet,' Mom said. 'First I'll have a look around myself. Hand me that baseball bat in the corner.'

'For what?' I asked.

'Just in case,' Mom said.

I gave Mom the bat. She held it like she was ready to use it. We waited until we heard the noise again. *Whooo . . . whooo . . . whooo . . .*

'That's coming from outside,' Mom said.

'So it's an outside ghost,' I told her.

She went to the window. She stood there for a minute before she started to laugh.

'What's funny?' I asked.

'Oh, Sheila . . . just look!'

I hid behind her and peeked out of the window. There was a beautiful silver moon. And there was also Jennifer, with her head held high. *She* was making those noises.

'What is she doing?' I asked. 'Is she crazy?'

'She's baying at the moon,' Mom said.

'What's baying?'

'It's like singing.'

'You mean she is going to stand there and make that ghost noise all summer?'

'I think so,' Mom said.

'I told you to get rid of her, didn't I?' I said. 'Who needs her? Who needs her making scary noises at me?'

'Come on, Sheila,' Mom said, putting the baseball bat back in the corner. 'Get into bed.'

She tucked me in. I felt very tired.

'Now go to sleep.'

'I'll try,' I said.

When Mom left I heard the noise again. *Whooo whooo whooo.*

'Oh shut up, you dumb old dog!' I called.

And she did.

Judy Blume

Unexpected charge of an enraged bull

Mouse and his friend Ezzie have thought of seventeen ways of coping with the type of emergencies seen frequently in films and on TV.

He lay with his eyes closed, trying to remember some more of the old ways he and Ezzie knew to survive life's greatest emergencies.

Emergency Three – Unexpected Charge of an Enraged Bull. Bulls have a blind spot in the centre of their vision, so when being charged by a bull, you try to line yourself up with this blind spot.

'Fat people can't do it, Mouse,' Ezzie had told him. 'That's why you never see any fat bull-fighters. You and I can. We just turn sideways like this, see, get in the blind spot and wait.'

He could remember exactly how Ezzie had looked, waiting sideways in the blind spot of an imaginary bull. 'And there's one other thing,' Ezzie had added. 'It will probably work for a rhinoceros too.'

Emergency Four – Crocodile Attack. When attacked by a crocodile, prop a stick in its mouth and the crocodile is helpless.

At one time this had been his own favourite emergency. He had spent a lot of time dreaming of tricking crocodiles. He had imagined himself a tornado in the water, handing out the sticks like party favours. 'Take that and that and that!' The stunned crocodiles, mouths propped open, had dragged themselves away. For the rest of their lives they had avoided children with sticks in their hands. 'Hey, no!' his dream crocodiles had cried, 'Let that kid alone. He's got sticks, man, *sticks!*'

Betsy Byars

Mortimer

All the things I am going to tell you now happened during one terrible, wild, wet week in February, when Mortimer the raven had been living with the Jones family in Rumbury Town, London N.W.3½ for several months. The weather had been so dreadful for so long that everybody in the family was, if not in a bad temper, at least less cheerful than usual.

Mrs Jones complained that even the bread felt damp unless it was made into toast, Arabel had the beginnings of a cold, Mr Jones found it very tiring to drive his taxi through pouring rain along greasy skiddy roads day after day, and Mortimer the raven was annoyed because there were two things he wanted to do, and he was not permitted to do either of them. He wanted to be given a ride round the garden on Arabel's red truck; Mrs Jones would not allow it because of the weather; and he wanted to climb into the bread bin and go to sleep there. It seemed to him highly unreasonable that he was not allowed to do this.

'We could keep the bread somewhere else,' Arabel said.

'So I buy a bread bin that costs eighty-seven-and-a-half pence for a great, black, sulky, lazy bird to sleep in? What's wrong with the coal-scuttle? He's slept in that for the last three weeks. So it's suddenly not comfortable any more?'

Mrs Jones had just come back from shopping, very wet; she began taking groceries and vegetables out of her wheeled shopping bag and dumping them on the kitchen floor. She hung her dripping umbrella beside the tea-towels.

'He wants a change,' Arabel said, looking out of the window at the grey lines of rain that went slamming across the garden like telephone wires.

'Oh, naturally! Ginger marmalade on crumpets that bird gets for his breakfast, spaghetti and meatballs for lunch, brandysnaps for supper, allowed to sit inside the grandfather clock whenever he wants, *and* slide down the stairs whenever he feels like it on my best wedding tray painted with pink and green gladioli, and he must have a change as well? That bird gets more attention than the Lord Mayor of Hyderabad.'

'*He* doesn't know that,' Arabel said. 'He's never been to Hyderabad.'

'So could we all do with a change,' said Mrs Jones. 'What's so particular about him that he should be one when the rest of us have to do without?'

Arabel and Mortimer went slowly away into the front hall. After a while Arabel picked up Mortimer, sat him on one of her roller-skates, tied a bit of string to it, and pulled him around the downstairs part of the house. But neither of them cheered up much. Arabel's throat felt tight and tickly. Mortimer knew all the scenery too well to be interested in the trip. He rode along with his head sunk down between his shoulders and his beak sunk down among his chest feathers, and his back and wing feathers all higgledy-piggledy, as if he didn't care which way they pointed.

The telephone rang.

Mortimer meant to get to it first – he loved answering the telephone – but he had one of his long toenails caught in the roller-skate. Kicking and flapping to free himself he started the skate rolling, shot through the hall door, across the kitchen, knocked over Mrs Jones's openwork vegetable rack, which had four pounds of brussels sprouts in the top compartment, and cannoned off that into a bag of coffee beans and a tall container of oven spray, which began shooting out thick frothy foam. Mrs Jones's umbrella fell off the towel-hanger and stabbed clean through a ripe melon which had rolled underneath. A fierce white smoke came boiling off the oven-spray which made everybody cough; Mrs Jones rushed to open the window. A lot of rain and wind blew in, knocking over a tall jar of daffodils that stood on the window-sill; Mortimer, who was interested in putting rough, knobbly things underneath flat, smooth things, began quickly sliding the daffodils (which were made of plastic) underneath the kitchen mat.

'Don't touch that foam!' said Mrs Jones, and she grabbed a large handful of paper towels and mopped it up. The telephone went on ringing.

Mortimer suddenly noticed the open window; he left the daffodils, climbed up the handles of the drawers under the kitchen sink, very fast, claw over claw, scrabbled along the edge of the sink, skated up the draining-board, hoisted himself up on the sill, and looked out into the wild, wet, windy garden.

'Drat that phone!' said Mrs Jones, mopped up the last of the foam, and rushed to the front hall. Just as she got there, the telephone stopped ringing.

Mortimer, leaning out of the window, saw that Arabel's red truck was down below on the grass, with half an inch of rain inside it. He jumped out.

'Mortimer!' said Arabel. 'Come inside! You'll get wet.'

Mortimer was wet already. He was loving it. He took no notice of Arabel.

There were half a dozen conkers floating in the red truck. The next-door cat, Ginger, was sitting under a holly-bush, trying to keep dry. Mortimer stood in the truck (the water came up to his knee-feathers) and began throwing conkers at Ginger.

'Mortimer!' said Arabel, hanging out of the window. 'You are not to throw conkers at Ginger. He's never done you any harm.'

Mortimer took no notice. He threw another conker.

Arabel wriggled back off the draining-board, opened the back door, ran out into the wet garden, grabbed the string of the truck, and pulled it back indoors, with Mortimer on board.

A good deal of the water slopped out on to the kitchen floor; it was like a tidal wave carrying the coffee beans and brussels sprouts towards the hall door.

Joan Aiken

CAMEL, hardly run in (3,000 miles), low fuel consumption, fully upholstered hump, will bite road hogs but won't desert you. Phone Ali on 1243.

Buying a pet

If you are going to buy a pet I would suggest a camel. They are not hard to feed and can be left for weeks at a time without water. They are ideal pets to keep if there is a drought. They don't need to be taxed or M.O.T.'d to go on the road and a lot of mileage can be obtained out of those strong, sturdy feet. Maintenance is practically unheard of and moving parts need not be oiled. When you go down the main road, if you don't get embarrassed, you can sit there with pride saying, 'Nothing better for economy.' A passenger can be taken on the back but this puts unnecessary weight on the vehicle.

When you pluck up enough courage to perch yourself on a hump you realize that the suspension is inadequate but rumours are that later models will be more luxurious.

You can take it into the living room and while watching TV you can stroke it or pat it as the mood takes you. If this does not appeal, how about giving it the garage with some straw scattered about. Your friends will envy you from the very first day you get the beast and before long the idea will catch on so that in the near future it will be a common sight to see these vehicles cruising down the M.1.

Kim Archer

Skeleton!

The blood that once ran through
the old creature's veins
has gone.
And all that is left is the
Silent, frightening, cream, cold bones.

The smile on the old rabbit's face
that seems to say
I'm glad that the blood poured
    from my wound
I am glad that they
pulled and tore me apart
and put me to stand in this
bare glass case.

Helen Moody

Goldfish

the scene of the crime
was a goldfish bowl
goldfish were kept
in the bowl at the time:

that was the scene
and that was the crime

Alan Jackson

I'm the hard one!

I'm the hard one;
The one who has a reputation to keep.
The one who leads the gang.
Takes the beatings and wins the beatings.
I'm the hard one;
The one what has earrings in his right ear and not his left.
The one that's six foot three inches and not three foot six
     inches.
I'm the hard one;
The one who looks after his gang if they're in trouble.
The one who's not scared of anybody,
Has dots on his knuckles, in other words,
Oy you, wanna scrap?
I'm the hard one;
The one that's got a lass every night of the week.
And the one that dreads that one day
He'll meet his match.
I'm the hard one.

John Gilbert

Round one ✓

I was not a one for fights, I must admit I cry very easily when I'm fighting. About two and a half years ago I was still in Ladybrook Primary School, my class was J2B. I was quite a soft boy who tried not to get into mischief. About half-way through the year, a boy called John Willet came to our school. He was small, medium build and he loved fighting. It wouldn't surprise me if it was his hobby. I stayed out of his way because I didn't want to get into a fight with him, even though I thought he was a little weakling. I could beat him. He was just a big head. But I didn't want to find out whether this was true.

A week after John had come, I was playing football with Paul Stobbs and James Simmons. 'Paul Stobbs kicked it out, Hardman collected, dribbled past Simmons, shot and SCORED!' We were happily playing football until John Willet came riding past and shouted 'Do you want a scrap?' Paul Stobbs replied 'I don't fight squirts like you.' Stupidly I said 'Yeah, you only weigh two stone.' There was a pause, then John threw down his bike and came running at us. I was not bothered until I saw he was running at me! A number of things went through my mind; I can't remember what. He started throwing punches at me. I was amazed by the power of them.

I thought I had an advantage because I had football boots on. We tripped each other up and started struggling on the

ground. While we were fighting, James had got John's bike and had run off with it. We didn't notice this happening because we were kicking the guts out of each other.

After about five minutes I started to cry; I don't know why, I just started to cry. John saw I was crying and stopped fighting me, thinking the battle had been won. He went back to get his bike, but it wasn't there. He told us if we didn't give him his bike back, he would get his big brother. This made me frightened. So James got his bike back for him. When John had gone we decided to call it a day.

When I got home I ran upstairs, and hid behind my bed until my tears ceased. I knew I had lost. Next day I didn't want to go to school. I was dropping hints I didn't feel very well, but in the end I went.

While I was walking to school, I was wondering what would John say; would he want a return fight? All these things passed through my mind. When I arrived, John wasn't there. I was hoping, wishing that he wouldn't come, but he did. I was expecting him to call me names and jeer at me but he didn't. When we were going into the mobile, John said to my amazement, 'Sorry about last night.' I replied 'It's O.K.' A boy who had overhead said 'What's the matter?' John replied, 'I beat him in.' When he said this I felt very small and like a weed. But one thing's certain: I live to fight another day.

Ian Hardman

61

Right!

Characters: Les, Tim

Outside

Les Hey you!
Tim Who? Me?
Les You I'm talking to. You.
Tim What?
Les Who do you think you're staring at?
Tim You what?
Les Who do you think you're looking at?
Tim I'm not looking at anybody.
Les You are. You're looking at me.
Tim I'm not.
Les You are. You're doing it now.
Tim Only 'cause you shouted. I wasn't looking before.
Les You were. You were staring.
Tim I wasn't.
Les You were.
Tim I wasn't.
Les Are you calling me a liar?
Tim No.
Les You are.
Tim I'm just telling you. I'm just saying, I wasn't looking at you. Honest.
Les So you're saying I'm a liar, then.
Tim No.
Les You'd better watch who you're calling a liar.
Tim I'm not.
Les You'd better look out, that's all.
Tim What for?
Les For me. You'd better look out for me.
Tim You said I hadn't to.
Les What?
Tim Look at you.
Les Are you trying to be funny?
Tim No.
Les Don't try to be funny with me.
Tim I wasn't. It was just a joke.
Les You'll not be laughing when I've finished with you.
Tim I'm not laughing. Who's laughing? I'm not.
Les You'll be laughing on the other side of your face. You don't mess with Les.
Tim Eh?
Les You don't mess with Les. What are you grinning at?
Tim I'm not. It's just the way my mouth is.
Les Right. Down the dene after school.
Tim Which dene?
Les What you mean, which dene? The dene.
Tim I don't go home that way.
Les You'd better be there.
Tim I've got the bus to catch.
Les Be there!
Tim Right!
Les Right!

David Williams

Nobody's putting me in no garbage can

One recess long ago the boys had decided to put some girls in the school trash cans. It had been one of those suggestions that stuns everyone with its rightness. Someone had said, 'Hey, let's put those girls over there in the trash cans!' and the plan won immediate acceptance. Nothing could have been more appropriate. The trash cans were big and had just been emptied, and in an instant the boys were off chasing the girls and yelling at the tops of their lungs.

It had been wonderful at first, Mouse remembered. Primitive blood had raced through his body. The desire to capture had driven him like a wild man through the school yard, up the sidewalk, everywhere. He understood what had driven the cave man and the barbarian, because this same passion was driving him. Putting the girls in the trash cans was the most important challenge of his life. His long screaming charge ended with him red-faced, gasping for breath – and with Viola Angotti pinned against the garbage cans.

His moment of triumph was short. It lasted about two seconds. Then it began to dim as he realized, first, that it *was* Viola Angotti, and, second, that he was not going to be able to get her into the garbage can without a great deal of help.

He cried, 'Hey, you guys, come on, I've got one,' but behind him the school yard was silent. Where was everybody? he had wondered uneasily. As it turned out, the principal had caught the other boys, and they were all being marched back in the front door of the school, but Mouse didn't know this.

He called again, 'Come on, you guys, get the lid off this garbage can, will you?'

And then, when he said that, Viola Angotti had taken two steps forward. She said, 'Nobody's putting *me* in no garbage can.' He could still remember how she had looked standing there. She had recently taken the part of the Statue of Liberty in a class play, and somehow she seemed taller and stronger at this moment than when she had been in costume.

He cried, 'Hey, you guys!' It was a plea. 'Where are you?'

And then Viola Angotti had taken one more step, and with a faint sigh she had socked him in the stomach so hard that he had doubled over and lost his lunch. He hadn't known it was possible to be hit like that outside a boxing ring. It was the hardest blow he had ever taken. Viola Angotti could be heavyweight champion of the world.

As she walked past his crumpled body she had said again,' 'Nobody's putting me in no garbage can.' It had sounded like one of the world's basic truths. The sun will rise. The tides will flow. Nobody's putting Viola Angotti in no garbage can.

Later, when he thought about it, he realized that he had been lucky. If she had wanted to, Viola Angotti could have capped her victory by tossing his rag-doll body into the garbage can and slamming down the lid. Then, when the principal came out on the playground calling, 'Benjamin Fawley! Has anybody seen Benjamin Fawley?' he would have had to moan, 'I'm in here.' He would have had to climb out of the garbage can in front of the whole school. His shame would have followed him for life. When he was a grown man, people would still be pointing him out to their children. 'That's the man that Viola Angotti stuffed into the garbage can.'

Betsy Byars

Philip Hall likes me. I reckon maybe

Mama set my morning bowl of steaming grits on the flowered oilcloth. 'I don't want no daughter of mine filling up her head with that Hall boy today. You get yourself some learning, Beth.'

I sprinkled some sugar on my grits and skimmed a spoonful from the top.

'You hear me a-speaking to you, girl?'

. . . Yes'm. But Philip Hall is my friend and –

Mama shook her head like it almost wasn't worthwhile explaining it to me. 'Beth, honey, you is so smart about most things. How come the good Lord made you so dumb about Philip Hall?'

'He didn't!' I said.

'Sure enough he did,' argued Mama. 'Don't you see he only wants your company if Gordy or one of them Jones boys ain't around and when he runs out of mischief to fall into?'

'Now that's not true,' I said, dropping my spoon noisily into the grits. ''Cause Philip Hall likes me. I reckon maybe. He's always inviting me over to his very own farm, now ain't that the truth?'

Ma pressed her hands against her wide waist. 'That is the very thing I is speaking about,' she said. 'He's got you cleaning out his dairy barn – doing his work!'

'Well, I don't mind a bit,' I told her. 'He strummed some songs on his guitar while I worked. It was nice.'

'You and your big sister better get on out of here, girl!' said Mama, wrapping her strong, dark arms around me. 'Or you both going to miss the school bus.' Her kiss made a smacking sound against my cheek. 'Now get!'

Outside, my Pa was throwing slop into the pig trough from a battered tin bucket. When he saw Anne, he called out, 'Euuuuu Wheee! Who that coming down the road in the starched-up dress?'

Annie smiled in that shy way she always does when she is being teased by the opposite sex. 'Oh, Pa . . .'

Then Pa looked at me and asked, 'Then somebody tell me who it is coming down the road in the faded jeans?'

'I reckon it's one of your two girl children. Want any more hints?'

'Oh, give me another little hint,' said Pa, letting his good, strong teeth show.

'I'm only the daughter that's the second-best arithmetic solver, the second-best speller, and the second-best reader in Miss Johnson's class.'

Pa wiped the sweat from his forehead with the sleeve of his denim shirt. 'That Hall boy again? Don't go telling me he's number-one best in everything.'

'Everything,' I said. 'Just everything.' And yet Pa's question started me wondering something I never wondered before. Is Philip Hall number one only 'cause I let him be? Afraid he wouldn't like me if I were best? Shucks no! And that's too silly to even think about.

The wind was a-blowing up the dust on the dry dirt road that ran between our pig and poultry farm and Mr Hall's dairy farm. A long time ago my mama showed me what to do when the road is dry from lack of rain and the wind comes up to make matters worse. Secret is to walk along the grass at the very edge of the road. Takes longer, but at least you can get to the highway clean.

Long after I had walked half-way, I spotted his shirt as red as dime-store lipstick. Up there where the dirt road meets up with the blacktop.

'Hey, Philip! Hey, hey, Phil-ip!'

He heard me because the shirt could be seen suddenly going down then up, down then up. He called out, 'Run! Run! Run!' As I came closer, I could see a coffee-coloured arm pointing down the road in the direction that the bus comes. 'Hur-ry, Hur-ry, the bus! THE BUS!'

'Let's run, Annie,' I said, hugging my lunchpail and books against my chest and taking off like a turkey on Thanksgiving Eve. My sister wasn't running with me. Well, let her miss the bus if she wants to. I ran even faster down the middle of the dusty road. Five miles to school is a heap of walking. Faster, I ran faster. Running made the dust rise higher and higher. I held by breath. But suddenly my mouth opened and I sucked in air – Ah-hm, Ahh-hmmm – and dust.

Philip's arms made wide circles. 'Come on, Beth. Come on. Come on!'

I had to go on. Couldn't disappoint him, not sweet Philip. Uhh chmm: Uhhhh chm! Made myself go. Made myself run. Uhhh hmm. Dust in my nose. My throat. Uhh uhhh!

As he wildly waved me on he shouted from the loudest part of his voice, 'BUS IS COMING! ALMOST HERE!'

Not much farther. I was going to make it. I had – 'Ohhhhh!' A speck of something struck my right eye. If only I could lie down in the fresh grass by the side of the road, wipe the speck from my eye, and breathe country air again. But I didn't lie down, didn't stop. Kept going . . . kept running until I reached . . . reached blacktop!

After I wiped the speck from my eye, I looked down, straight down that long, black-topped road, but I didn't see anything. 'Where . . . where's the bus?' I asked Philip while struggling to get back my breath.

Philip looked very serious – no, he didn't. He was biting his lip, trying to hold a straight face. Suddenly his lip came unbit. 'Ah ha ha ha. Did I fool you! You just a-running down that road. Ah ha ha ha!'

'Why! Why! . . . You . . . you no good, low-down polecat!'

Philip looked surprised. 'Can't you take a joke?'

I thought about shoving him into the gully at the side of the road. 'That's not one bit a joke, Philip Hall. What that is is mean. Low-down mean!'

'Awww, I thought you was one girl could take a joke.'

'I can!' I said, brushing the dust off me as best I could. 'Just as good as anybody.'

Philip nodded. 'For a girl, you take jokes better than anybody.' Suddenly he pointed down the road and this time the yellow bus was really on its way. He smiled a dimpled smile and I remembered why he's the cutest boy in the J. T. Williams School.

Mr Barnes squeaked the bus to a stop and opened the door to let Fancy Annie first on board. When I got on, my friend Bonnie called, 'Sit next to me, Beth.'

I was just about to tell her that I had already promised to sit next to Philip Hall when I saw him slide into the seat next to Gordon. The dumb bum.

'Hey, Phil,' said Gordon. 'First thing this morning old Henry brought your invitation.'

'Philip must be having another birthday party,' whispered Bonnie. 'Reckon he'll invite us?'

'Philip Hall likes me,' I told her. 'Most every day after my chores, I go over to his farm and he sings and just plays his guitar for me. And later this day, when old Henry get around to our house, I reckon I'll have my invitation too.'

Then Bonnie, who mostly acts as though she invented talking, stopped talking. Something had to be upsetting her, and I knew what it was. 'Now don't you fret,' I told her. 'Maybe Philip Hall will invite you too.'

'But what if he doesn't?' she asked, becoming more upset.

'Then, in that case,' I told her, 'don't you worry none. 'Cause you is my friend and he is my friend and I'll just tell him to invite you 'cause you is my friend.'

At recess I told Susan, Ginny, and Esther about the invitation that was waiting for me. They all said that they wanted one too, and I told them all not to fret. 'Cause if they wanted to go, then I'd only have to ask Philip to invite them.

When the last bell of the day rang, I was the first one out of the classroom and the third in line for the bus. Mr Barnes isn't too good about waiting for kids and, anyway, Philip likes me to save him a place.

'Hey, Philip,' I called, at the first sight of red shirt. 'Over here.'

Gordon looked at Philip as though he was clear out of his mind. 'You let a girl save places for you? She your girlfriend, Phil?'

His face crinkled into a dark frown. 'She's *not* my girlfriend. And I *hate* girls!'

I climbed on the bus, without once even looking at that dumb bum who spent the whole trip back laughing with Gordon and telling him about the food they were going to eat and the games they were going to play at his birthday party. And Philip Hall is not one bit the cutest boy in school either, and that's for sure.

Where our dirt road meets the blacktop, Mr Barnes brought the bus to a stop and Anne, Philip, and I jumped off. As my boyfriend no more and I poked along the dirt road together, I wasn't saying one word to him. Finally, he said something to me, 'Afternoon shower dampened the road down. Ain't one bit dusty now.'

'Reckon I'm not going to talk to you about any damp roads or any dusty roads or any kind of roads at all.'

Philip dimpled a smile. 'Oh, you is mad, Beth Lambert. You is mad, Mad, MAD! Ain't that right?'

'That is right, Mister Philip best-in-the-class Hall. You all the time rather be sitting with Gordon and laughing with Gordon and telling him that I'm not your friend. And that makes me mad. Mad. Mad. MAD!'

Philip reached up and pulled a leaf from an elm, 'You is my friend all right.'

'I am . . . truly?'

Philip looked down at his shoes and nodded. 'Sure. 'Cause after you finish up the chores on your farm, I'm going to let you come visit. I'm going to let you brush down my cows.'

'See you directly,' I called as I started running to catch up with Anne. My chores shouldn't take long. And then probably I could go over to Philip Hall's. Sweet Philip. I had to get him something very special for his eleventh birthday. What?

Suddenly I knew. A pick for his guitar just like they sell at the Busy Bee Bargain Store. And with the nickel I had saved from not buying ice-cream last Saturday, together with the nickel that Pa will give me this Saturday, then I'd have a whole dime to spend on a guitar pick for sweet Philip Hall.

Mama was sitting on her porch chair, rocking away. Near her feet was the big sewing basket and in her lap was Pa's old overalls that was getting fresh knee patches.

'Hey, Ma, old Henry brought the mail yet?'

She looked up from her sewing. 'Mail's on the kitchen table.'

Behind me, I heard the screen door slam. Mama don't like no screen door slamming. On the oilcloth-covered table was a platter of fried chicken, a pot of still warm black-eyed peas, and a catalogue for mail ordering. This ain't all the mail. Can't be!

I went back into the living-room, which is also my brother Luther's bedroom, and hollered through the screen door, 'Ma, this ain't all the mail . . . is it?'

She was quiet for a moment and I thought she was about to say that was all there was when; 'N-o-o-o,' she called back, 'reckon not. There's something else on my bureau.'

I knew it. I just knew it! But when I looked the only piece of mail I saw was a circular announcing bargain day at the Busy Bee. Maybe the invitation is underneath. Sure. My hand touched the sheet of advertisement without really moving it. I hope, I hope. I lifted the circular. And there was – nothing! Absolutely nothing.

I tiptoed out the kitchen door, closing it without a sound. Crossed the dirt road, shortcutted through the cornfield and passed the mailbox where the sign read: HALL'S DAIRY. Inside the barn Philip was sitting on a bale of hay, picking out a tune on his guitar.

Without even looking up from his guitar strings, he said, 'You better get busy, Beth. You got eight milk cows to brush down today.'

'You didn't send me one.' My voice sounded right next door to tears.

Philip took notice. 'What? Send you –

'A birthday invitation,' I said. 'Sent one to Gordon, but not to me.'

'Oh,' said Philip. 'That. That's what you mad about?'

I nodded while tears stung at my eyes. 'I was going to buy you a special present 'cause I thought you was my friend, but you're not my friend at all.'

'Don't be like that,' he said. 'I didn't invite girls, only Gordy, Bobby, and Jordan and Joshua Jones – the brave members of the 'Tiger Hunters' Club. We're the boys ain't afraid of nothing. Not even roaring mad tigers.'

'Well, why couldn't you invite me too? I'm not even a little bit afraid of tigers either and you said . . . this very day, you said I was your friend.'

Philip nodded his head yes.

'So why didn't you invite me too?'

'. . . I can't.'

'Well why not?'

'Just can't.'

'Why *not*?'

'Just *can't* do it.'

'W*hy*?'

'' 'cause.'

'' 'cause *why*?'

'' 'cause . . . 'cause I was afraid they'd call me sissy. Then they'd go 'round saying I liked you and that you was my girlfriend, stuff like that.'

'And you the president of the Tiger Hunters?' I asked. 'That the club ain't afraid of nothing, not even roaring mad tigers?' I began to laugh.

Philip looked frightened. 'What you laughing at?'

I only laughed some more.

'Are you laughing at me?'

'Reckon I is 'cause you is funny, Funny, FUNNY, Mister Philip Hall.'

'I'm not! Not! NOT!' shouted Philip, jumping off the bale of hay.

'Oh, yes you is. You say you ain't afraid of tigers. Well, I don't know a soul ever seen a tiger, not in all of Randolph County. But you is afraid of a word, and everybody knows that words can't bite and words can't scratch. So you're not a tiger hunter, Philip Hall. What you is, is a 'fraidy cat. And that's a whole lot worse than being a sissy.'

Bette Greene

Too much water

It is 1949 and the heroine of Knock and Wait, *who is never named, has been sent for a year from her home in Nottinghamshire to an Open Air School in Kent in an attempt to cure her anaemia.*

It was like being in a railway station in that Sick Bay because I'd only taken a single bite of my bread and jam when Sister Sweet comes charging back with this new girl. 'It's a wonder you ever got here,' Sister Sweet is shouting and this new girl doesn't say a word, just looks at me and grins and I just keep looking at her. I don't feel like smiling at anybody and, when I don't smile back, this girl sticks out her tongue, puts her thumb to the end of her nose and waggles her fingers at me. I think, cor blimey, this is just like home and I feel better straight away.

Sister Sweet went flying out again after telling this new girl to get undressed and when she'd gone, this lass turns to me and says, 'I'm Golda Miranda and I come from London and I hate it here. Do you?' and I says, 'Yes.'

'How long you been here then?' she says and I tell her I've only just come. 'Rotten old place, innit?' Golda says and I nod my head. 'How long you here for then?' she goes on, and I say, 'A year,' and she says, 'I'm here for thirty-two million seconds,' and I says to her, 'That's a year as well,' and she says 'Yers,' and then we both shut up.

Golda Miranda gets changed into her night clothes and drinks her cocoa and eats her bread and jam and then she says to me, 'Are you crying?' because water was running down my face.

'No,' I says. 'What do you think I am, a cry baby or something?' and she says, 'Oh, all right, keep your hair on. I was only asking.'

I told her I never cried and when tears ran down my face it was only because I'd been drinking too much water.

Our Joe told me about that. It was when he fell off a tree once and he'd hurt himself and these tears started running down his face. 'Are you crying, our Joe?' I asked him and he hit me and said, 'Stupid! Course I'm not crying. Lads don't cry,' and I said to him, 'What are those tears on your face, then?'

'Tears!' he said. 'You call them tears. I'll tell you what they are. I've been drinking too much water, that's what they are.'

'If you drink too much water, does it come out of your eyes then?' I asked him, and he said 'Course it does. Has to go somewhere, dun it? It's like when you pour a cup of tea. If you put too much in the cup, it spills over. Well, that's what happens when you drink too much water. It goes up and up your body until it reaches your eyes, and then, because eyes are holes in your face, it comes out, trickle, trickle, trickle. That's what's on my face now. Water.'

I asked our Joe how you knew when you were really crying and he said I'd know. He didn't tell me how, but I always have known. Usually I'm not crying but have been drinking too much water.

Golda Miranda said she'd have to remember that about the water and did cocoa count?. I said I thought it did. Next minute, crash goes the door and there's Sister Sweet staring at us with her big purple face and she's going, 'Well! Well! Come along, girls. On your feet,' and me and this London lass stand up.

'Down to the bathroom,' Sister Sweet says and when we get out into the corridor, she goes, 'Oh, good heavens,' – point, point – 'it's straight down the corridor. Last door on the left.' Me and this Golda walk down into the bathroom and there's the nurse who brought us our cocoa and bread and jam. Nurse Jones, she says her name is. 'Ah,' she says. 'Get a move on, girls. Let's have the first one in.'

Golda looks round the bathroom and you can hardly see a thing because of the steam. 'Blimey,' she says. 'What they gonna do? Boil us alive.'

I says to her, 'I had a bath this morning and I had one last night as well. Many more and there'll be nothing of me left to wash at all.' Golda went, 'Oh, I know all about hospitals. All they ever think about is bathing you.'

This bath was a long white one, not like our grey tin one at home. It was very high and very, very deep and I can't swim. When I looked in it, I saw the water was *white*. I said to Nurse Jones, 'I've never seen white water before, missis,' and she said, 'It has disinfectant in it.' I says to her, 'I don't need no disinfecting. I'm a clean girl,' and she said, 'All new girls have to have a bath in disinfected water when they first arrive.'

'I'm not getting in there,' I said, and she said, 'Why not?'

'Only dirty people get disinfected,' I told her and she said, 'It's because of all the trains and buses you've been in today. They're not very clean and your mother wouldn't like it if we let you catch something nasty out of a dirty train, would she?'

I looked at her and she looked at me and then I said, 'Oh, all right.' I took off my things and put one foot in and went, 'Aaaagh!' Nurse Jones said, 'Whatever's wrong now?' I lifted my foot out of the water and it was bright red. Steaming bright red it was. 'Look at that,' I says. 'Look at my foot. It's been nearly boiled,' and the nurse went, 'Ha! Ha! What a funny girl you are,' and then said, 'Get in.'

'It's too hot,' I said. 'Honest, missis. It's red hot,' and she tutted a bit and put about four drops of cold water into the bath, out of a *tap*, not out of a bucket. They had taps at the end of the bath, just like on the pictures. When I got in again, it was still red hot and I watched all my feet and ankles go bright red all over again. Then, this nurse, she picked up a big brown scrubbing-brush and *started scrubbing me*.

Golda said, 'You're not doing that to me,' and Nurse Jones said, 'It doesn't hurt, does it?' to me, and I went, 'Ugh, ouch, no, ugh, ouch!' Golda looked at me and said, 'Are you sure it doesn't hurt?' and I shook my head because I couldn't open my mouth otherwise I would have screamed the place down.

Golda said, 'Oh, all right then,' and when it was her turn she got in and, as soon as the scrubbing-brush touched her, she yelled blue murder. 'I thought you said it didn't hurt,' she shouts at me. 'Just wait till I get out of here,' and I felt better than I had done since I left our house and grinned at her. But not for long, because all of a sudden the bathroom door smashed open and bashed against the wall and there was Sister Sweet standing in the doorway.

'Dreadful child!' she roared, and Nurse Jones looked as if she were going to faint. Sister Sweet shouted at her, 'Nurse! If you can just once do a job right I would be extremely grateful,' and Nurse Jones got all tears in her eyes. I don't think she'd been drinking too much water either, and Golda looked at her and then at Sister Sweet and just shut up.

When Golda got out of the bath, Sister Sweet stared hard at her and said, 'I shall be keeping a special eye on you two girls,' and swung her head round so she could stare at me as well. Golda went, 'Ugh,' – mutter, mutter – and Sister Sweet roared, 'Don't answer me back, you impertinent child,' and Golda went, 'Ugh,' – mutter, mutter – again. I could see Sister Sweet's face going more and more purple, like the plums we used to pinch off this fellow's tree at home, and I saw her great big red hand reach out for Golda and I nipped in front of her and went, 'Ohhhhhh,' and slowly fell on the floor.

I learnt how to do that at dancing class. Miss Brown taught me. Sister Sweet's hand stopped in mid-air and she whipped round and grabbed a big white towel and picked me up and wrapped it round me and rushed me back into the Sick Bay and threw me onto the bed, as if I were only a nightgown and not a girl at all. Then, she stuck this long glass thing in my mouth and all at once I thought, I don't care about anything any more, and Sister Sweet said, 'You girls! You never learn. You're all the same.' Then she took this glass thing out of my mouth, wrote something on a bit of paper which was on a board clipped to the bottom on the bed and went out. I was glad to see her go.

Golda came in then, snarling and moaning and groaning, and jumped into bed. The nurse came and saw to her, then switched off the light and went out, leaving the door half open.

This Golda whispers, 'Do you think Sister Sweet looks like a gorilla?'

Gwen Grant

Billy's game

Once outside a few younger children gave him a second glance as they ran past to form their groups and start their games. But of the boys in his own class there was no sign at first, until the sight of an arching ball above the asbestos kitchen told him there was a playing space beyond. He tried to walk round to it, but impatience forced him into a run, to stop just short of the corner, and, with a carefully prepared expression, neither over-eager nor too tightly closed, to stroll casually round.

The game was being played against a short length of clear brick wall upon which a small goal had been painted, with the unnecessary word GOAL in the centre. The teams were exclusively boys from his own class, with Billy between the flat whitewashed posts. It was a one-ended game, attackers and defenders playing into the one goal, and Billy seemed to be dominating it, loudly claiming every ball remotely within reach as his.

Paul stopped and put his own ball on the ground between his feet. With Billy being kept so busy, there'd be no chance of being invited into this.

They weren't all that good, Paul decided; if these boys were to be in the school team then he should make it, too. But Billy was a skilful goalie, and it was obvious that the whole game was organized the way it was purely for his benefit. When the three goals had been scored (Paul noticed that it took five to get three, since Billy disallowed two good goals as being on the post) the attackers and the defenders changed position, but Billy remained in the goal. It was a good job he played on pitch himself, Paul thought. There'd be no competing with this boy.

Billy was tall without being skinny, athletic looking, and smartly dressed in a red track-suit top and jeans. He had the sort of fair hair that didn't ruffle in the heat of the game, but fell back into place naturally, and only his reddening face gave an indication of his strenuous exertions to keep the ball out. The shouting did that, too, calling the odds, abusing the other boys for poor play, the tirade of words issuing from a thin mouth that twisted them out as if what he was shouting was really meant to be confidential. It was as if he was confiding his disgust in them at the top of his voice. The others, probably having given in to him since they'd first been infants, allowed him his own way in all things, apologizing for bad balls when Billy couldn't get to them, running and getting them for goalie's kicks when they went over the wall into the coke pile, complimenting him on almost every touch. Paul's spirits sank, He'd never get into this closed set-up! and even if he did, he was sure he couldn't take all that grovelling round Billy.

In no time the whistle went; Mrs Lewis, the senior infant teacher, no lover of boisterous break-times with the juniors, gave a specially loud blast round their private corner to get the fourth-year game to end. But Paul decided to stay where he was for a moment. Billy would have to walk past him to get into school, and a sort of fatal fascination held Paul there to see what would happen. The tall boy could either walk past him, absorbed with his group, and pretend not to see him, or he could stop and say something, perhaps try to recruit a new follower.

With his own red ball under his arm Billy came towards him, listening to someone complimenting him on a save. It was clearly in his mind to ignore Paul, until he saw the ball in Paul's arms. It certainly took his eye up close. Still unkicked, it did look attractive, smooth white with sharp black lettering.

'That a Frido ball, son?' Without asking, he took it from Paul's hands and pressed it professionally with his thumbs, like a First Division goalie before a match.

'Yeah. Cup Final Special.' Paul didn't reach out to get it back. He dropped his hands and waited for Billy to finish admiring it.

Billy bounced it hard on the ground twice.

'Regulation weight?'

Paul nodded. 'Yeah. Proper ball, only plastic . . .' It had been a good move, then, bringing the new ball.

Billy still held it. 'Thought so.' Then he suddenly changed the subject. 'Didn't I see you yesterday over the park?'

Paul nodded again. Billy must have been one of the boys kicking about behind the goal. Well, it had shown his own keenness in the game, watching the match to the end the way he had.

'Hanging round the other team, London Docks, wasn't you? Eating their oranges?'

Paul stared back at him. The *other* team? Did there always have to be a catch? How was he to know who was who.? It hadn't been deliberate disloyalty to the estate.

'Thought so.'

Without warning, Billy dropped the ball at his feet and back-heeled it away from the group, back towards the vacant goal.

'Can't use that 'ere,' he said. 'Too 'eavy for the windows. School rule . . .'

He walked away in the midst of his giggling group, the king surrounded by his fawning court, self-important, confident in his leadership. Paul's spirits dropped into his boots as he walked over to get his ball. It was the final stoop to pick it up that got him, that made his eyes prick, like a beaten goalkeeper bending to retrieve it from the back of the net. He forced himself into a trot back into school, twenty metres behind the last girl, and as he ran he thought of the crowd that he would normally have been in, surrounding Simon Tulip. He thought of the gaggle of laughs, and the thumps, and the loud clever remarks – just what Billy was enjoying right now.

And suddenly he wanted it back like he'd never wanted anything in his life.

Bernard Ashley

69

Monkey

Porky, Chesty, Ear'ole, Israel, Darkie, Grandpa, Pongo, Rubberneck, Tiptoe, Ding-dong, Bug, Freddie-the -Fly, Professor, Snotty, Baggy and Scratcher Dan.

Depending on his habits, his proper name, his infirmities, his disposition, or his physical attributes, so each boy was nicknamed. Porky was a fat boy, Chesty a wheezer at night. Ear'ole had a mangled ear and Grandpa a hairy face. Israel was no anti-semitic tag – the boy's surname was Hands and we had all read *Treasure Island*. Professor was studious, Pongo insanitary; Rubberneck had a mechanical movement of that joining part of his anatomy, so he moved like a tortoise, and Scratcher Dan just scratched.

The staff had names too. There were Korky, Chuck, Jessie and Rumbletum – and they were all women. Successive and oft-changing assistant masters were in the gallery as Marlow, Little Affie, Slinger and Walrus.

The day after I arrived at the Kingston home from Woodford I was nicknamed. They called me Monkey. I went into the dormitory on the second night and there was a reception committee sitting on the beds. They wouldn't let me go past so I stood, trembling inside, looking at them.

As boys go they looked villainous enough. Jerseys, blue and grey, patched all over, trousers embroidered in the same way, socks around ankles and bursting shoes.

' 'lo Monkey,' said one kid standing in my way.

'Trying to be funny?' I said.

'Yeah, Monkey,' he grinned. 'Let's see you swing on the beams.'

The others all laughed and I knew I was going to have to have a fight. 'What do they call you, then?' I said to the spokesman. 'Is it Ape? Or Chimp?'

He hit me on the side of the head with a sharp, stony fist. I thought he'd knocked my eye out of its socket. I went straight over the iron bedrail and landed in the hard valley between two beds. My head was screaming and I could hear them all roaring around and above me. I heard someone shrieking 'A fight! The new kid's 'aving a fight!' From the next dormitory came a deluge of booted onlookers.

I knew I'd have to get up and I knew just as certainly that he would put me on my back again. Having caught me with the sudden swing, he now pranced about at the end of the beds between which I lay, shadow boxing and yelling to me to rise and fight him. At that moment I couldn't even focus him too well, but I thought he was no bigger than me. It was just that he'd hit me first.

'Come on out, Monkey,' he yelled. 'Let's see your monkey face.'

My leg must have been sticking out because he got hold of it and pulled me out. They were leaping on the beds, and shouting and laughing. It was like being in a cave with them all calling down at me.

The fighter got hold of my foot again. My shoe came off and he staggered back against one of the beds. When he came back I was up to meet him. I never could fight. But I was bristling with tears and temper. I ran at him and felt the top of my head crunch his nose. He swore in short words. Now I was there I hit him with both fists, my bony elbows and caught him a cruel thrust with my pointed knee.

He was on the ground and I was on him, my angry fingers on his hair, banging his head against the ground. His nose was discharging like a red river. In the end they pulled me off and in the true manner of boys carried me away in noisy glory while they left him to bleed.

I might have won my fight but I had not gained my point. Even in the flush of victory they were calling: 'He's won! Monkey's won! Good old Monkey! Good old Monkey!

Leslie Thomas

Signed: Your friend

On his way to school Bernard Kershaw sees Bobby Whitehead and Patsy Broome planning to attack some small Pakistani children. Just as the stones start to fly, Shofiq Rahman comes whirling a piece of rubber hose about his head. He routs the gang and flattens Bobby Whitehead.

In school, however, Bobby Whitehead claims to have been unjustifiably attacked. Bernard, despite his fear of Whitehead and his suspicion of the Pakistani children, stands up for Shofiq.

Since his mate Mickie had got himself squashed on the railway, Bernard had been at a loose end, to be quite honest. He had the gang, fair enough. But what did it all add up to, when all was said? There was Terry, who was smart enough, and didn't get cold feet if they had the odd brush with the Glossop Street lot, and didn't always go whining home to his mum if he fell off a wall and cut himself. He was all right, but he was a nuisance too, in some ways. His brother was in the Air Force cadets, and played in the band on Sunday mornings, and Terry was always going off and hanging around him, in case he got a go at banging the big drum, or helping fly the model planes and that. You couldn't depend on Terry.

Then there was Maureen and Dougie McIlroy. Now Maureen was all right, she was smashing. He'd been in love with Maureen, and they'd done kissing and all that sort of stuff; but since they'd got over it, mostly, she'd been even better. She could fight any lad of her own age and she didn't scratch or bite, neither. She'd socked him once, when he'd said her baby brother looked like a monkey, and she'd made his nose bleed. She wasn't bad.

Dougie though. He was a different matter. He was big, and a bit slow, and a cry-baby. He'd tag along, and do all the things Bernard told him to, but he just wasn't any fun. If they were in the buildings, say, and a grown-up shouted at them, or a cop car went past ten streets away, he'd quite likely burst into

tears, or hide, or scarper off home sharpish. Maureen bashed him about some, but even that was no satisfaction, because she wouldn't let anyone else have a go. He was right at the bottom of the class, and Bernard thought on the sly that he was a trifle on the backward side. All in all, he was a bit of a pain.

As a gang, let's face it, it was a dead loss.

[. . .]

Bernard was jerked back to the present by Miss Todd repeating his name.

'Bernard,' she said, sharply. 'Have you been listening? I said you can help your friend Shofiq hand out the Scripture books and collect in the pencils.'

'Yes, Miss. Sorry Miss,' he said, looking all bright and interested. This was her soft way of giving you a treat, letting you hand out books. He caught Maureen's eye, and he winked. But she was looking at him in a funny way. He realized what Miss had said. 'Your friend Shofiq.'

[. . .]

This lad, this Pakistani lad, owed him plenty. He'd saved his life. You'd think he'd show it somehow, show his gratitude. As they passed again, Bernard looked him full in the face and smiled. It was a daft smile, a false smile. It felt uncomfortable on his mouth. The big brown eyes looked into his.

'Hiya,' said Bernard lamely.

''Ello, lad,' replied Shofiq Rahman. 'Thanks.'

He'd said it! Bernard went back to his table blushing furiously. He was trembling inside. That Paki lad had said thanks! As he sat there staring blankly at his page of Scripture, all sorts of ideas formed in his head. New ideas,

great ideas. If he let him join the gang, they could do all sorts of things. He vividly remembered the flailing helicopter, it had been great. And although he never said much, Bernard knew he was not a dummy, he was good at all his subjects, better than most of the kids, better than Bernard at some things, and he made ace models in handicrafts, really smart things.

Over the next hour or two he dreamed happily of dangerous deeds undertaken, fantastic exploits achieved. Some of the things he'd done with Mickie, like hunting for gold, or climbing up the inside of the Raven Mill chimney when they'd broken open the boilershed during Wakes, some of the things that the gang ought to do but somehow he could never get them round to it any more. Most of all he dreamed about routing Bobby Whitehead and that crow Patsy Broome. Let alone them filling him in for telling on them over the business that morning, he'd be able to chase them from hell to breakfastime, as his dad would say. He'd get a lump of hosepipe too, and they could both be helicopters. They'd put the fear of Jiminy up them; that Whitehead would never be the same lad.

Problem was, how was he going to get hold of this Shofiq and sort it all out? In the muck-up at the end of the afternoon he might just lose him. Miss Todd had this potty way of sending them all out in batches, so she never had the trouble some of the teachers had over noise, and thundering hordes of kids all pelting down the corridors at once. And you never knew which batch you were going to be in. That was crafty too – it meant if someone was planning to batter someone they never knew if they'd get the chance – and old Toddy seemed to have a good idea on who wanted to bash who, as well. All in all, she was a rotten nuisance was Miss Toddy, a real strictie

In the end, he decided to send a note. Although they were meant to be doing quiet reading at this point, he had no trouble getting a bit of paper hidden down beside his book and a little stub pencil out of his pocket. He sucked it for a minute or two, waiting for inspiration, then decided on the dead straight approach.

'Dear Shoffeek.' Point one: he didn't know how to spell his rotten name! He guessed that was near enough though.

'If Miss sends you out before me could you hang about so I can see you urgent, it is imperative I see you. If she sends me out before you I will do same. Do not speak to anyone about this it is imperative secresy is maintained.'

That was that, almost. But it was the almost that was the hard part. How should he sign it?

Bernard pondered for a long time, not forgetting to flick over the page of his book every now and then; Bernard the Black Hand was a highly-trained spy, a match for any old teacher, even Miss Cat's Eyes Todd. His mind drifted back to the morning – the flailing hosepipe, the hail of bricks, the screaming kids, the beautiful sight of Shofiq Rahman laying low the terrible Bobby Whitehead. He made up his mind.

He sucked the pencil and wrote heavily: 'Signed: Your friend Bernard Kershaw.'

Jan Needle

Edith

Her name was Edith.

I did not like her. Edith always came to school with her clothes unpressed, her stockings bagging about her legs with big holes, which she tried to hide by pulling them into her shoes but which kept slipping up, on each heel, to expose a round, brown circle of dry skin the size of a quarter. Of course there were many children in this class that were untidy and whom I did not like. Some were tough. So tough that I was afraid of them. But at least they did not have to sit right across the aisle from me. Nor did they try to be friendly as Edith did – whenever she happened to come to school.

Edith walked into the classroom at late morning, causing the teacher to stop in the middle of one of her monotonous sentences to fasten a hate-filled glare, which Edith never saw, on her back.

'Good afternoon, Miss Jackson,' the teacher's voice, thick with sarcasm, followed her to her seat. But Edith, popping bubble gum on her back teeth so that it distorted her square little face, slammed her books on the desk, slipped her wiry body into her seat, then turned her head around the room nodding greetings to friends.

The teacher's voice rose sharply: 'It seems to me that if you *had* to honour us with your presence today, you could at least have been preparing yourself to come to class looking presentable.'

Her words had more effect on the class than on Edith. They always did. When I had first come into class I had thought it was because the teacher was white. Later I realized that it was because of the manner she spoke to the pupils. Now, the shuffle of feet sounded around the room, a banging of desks. The teacher shrilled: 'I am talking to you, Edith Jackson.'

'Huh, what? – oh, you talking to me? Good afternoon, Miss Lass.' Edith grinned with open-faced innocence. The teacher reddened. Edith turned her impish grin to include all of the appreciative snickers around the room. She then leaned across the aisle and said to me: 'Hi ya doin', Phyllisia?'

I pulled myself tall in my seat, made haughty little movements with my shoulders and head, adjusted the frills on the collar of my well-ironed blouse, touched my soft neatly plaited hair and pointedly gave my attention to the blackboard.

Edith ignored my snub. She always ignored my snubs. Edith had made up her mind, from the first day I entered this class, that she would be my friend whether I wanted it or not. 'Ain't it a pretty day out?' She grinned and made a loud explosion with her gum. 'Sure hated to come and stick myself in this dingy-ass classroom.'

A scene from Thames Television's version of extracts from **The Friends** *by Rosa Guy.*

Her words pulled my attention away from the blackboard and to the window where the sun came splashing into the room.

Since my father had sent for us, my sister Ruby who is sixteen and me, two years younger, and set us down in this miserable place called Harlem, New York, this was the first warm day. I, too, had not wanted to come here today. Walking to school, seeing people coming out of their homes with faces softened by smiles, for the first time I had been filled with the desire to run off somewhere, anywhere but to this room. I had not wanted to have to listen to a teacher I did not like, nor to sit among children I liked even less. But where could I go? I knew nothing about this strange city. Going one block out of my way between home and school, and I would be lost. And so I had come, grudgingly, but I had come.

Yet the moment I had entered the classroom, I knew that my instincts had been right. I should not have come today. The same recklessness that had pulled at me in the streets was big in the room, pulling and tugging at the control of the students. Fear cut a zigzag pattern from my stomach to my chest: The students in the class did not like *me*.

They mocked my West Indian accent, called me names – 'monkey' was one of the nicer ones. Sometimes they waited after school to tease me, following me at times for several blocks, shouting. But it had been cold and after a time they had been only too glad to hunch their shoulders up to their ears and go home. Winter, as much as I hated it, had protected me. Now it was spring.

Rosa Guy

I'll tell your mum

When he got to the hole in the hedge he met John, coming the other way. John went through the hole first, because he always did everything first, and pushed Steven into the hedge.

'Where've you been?' said John.

'In the field,' said Steven.

'No you haven't' said John. 'You've been down the river.'

'I never,' said Steven.

'I bet you have,' said John. That was better. If John was betting it meant that he didn't know. Or perhaps he did know, which was why he thought it was safe to bet.

·'I've been in the field.'

'Why you got water weed on your boots, then?' said John. Steven picked off the green ribbon of weed and threw it away. 'It's a good thing your mum never saw that. Shall I tell her, then?'

'Tell her what?'

'Tell her you been down the river. She'll belt you.' John bounced up and down on his toes, blocking the hole in the hedge.

'No,' said Steven. 'Don't tell her.'

'What'll you give me if I don't tell her?' said John. 'What have you got? When d'you get your pocket money? Eh? Eh?'

'Tomorrow,' said Steven.

'You going to give me any? Eh? Eh?' said John, bouncing harder than ever.

'Let me through. My mum'll come looking for me,' said Steven.

'I'll tell her where you been, then, shall I?' said John. 'Eh?'

'I'll show you my raft,' said Steven, and immediately wished that he hadn't. It would have been less trouble to part with his pocket money.

'You never got a raft,' said John. 'Your mum wouldn't let you. She won't let you go down the river, case you fall in.' Bounce, bounce, bounce. He had seen boxers do it, on the telly.

'I have got a raft,' said Steven.

'Don't believe you.'

'I'll show you tomorrow.'

'I'll go and see it now.'

'I hid it.'

'You? You couldn't hide an ant,' said John, up on his toes again. 'You couldn't hide a flea. You couldn't hide a *germ*!'

'I camouflaged it,' said Steven.

'I bet I find it. I'll go and find it now. I'll smash it up,' said John, watching Steven to see if he would cry.

Just then John s mother looked through the hole in the hedge. She thought that they were playing a nice game, and smiled at Steven.

'Are you coming in for tea, Johnny?' she said, and John said 'Yes, Mum.'

He followed her back to his house and went indoors, looking ever so good. John's mum wouldn't let him go to the river, either, and Steven knew that the raft was safe for tonight.

Jan Mark

74

The hand

I dragged out the old box to reach a magazine, but a side split and a pile of metal and plastic poured over the worn carpet. I went to shovel it back into the box, making a note to get rid of it all. Then I stopped; a small piece of dirty pink rubber lay before me: the gripping hand.

I had been at John's and my Action Man was ready for combat, clasping his Sterling with anticipation. John had set up camp and the ammunition and supplies were being packed into the jeep before the mission began at 1600 hours. I frowned in annoyance, for my soldier's gun had dropped from his plastic hands. The mission had to be delayed.

'Tell you what, I'll give you my mortar and a Sterling if I can have your gripping hands.'

'Dunno, I only just got them.'

'What if I give you a pair of boots as well?'

'Done!'

We exchanged equipment and were ready for battle.

The icy wind lashed the stinging rain onto the potato patch, where an enemy minefield confronted our commandos . . .

After the war my mother took me home.

With enthusiasm I showed her the gripping hands and explained the swop, waiting for approval. Instead she went to the phone and I sat down on the kitchen step knowing who she was phoning. Soon she replaced the receiver and turned to me.

'I'm going to take you back to John's and you're to return his things, and he will return yours.'

'But we're both happy with the swop, I . . .'

'Yes, I'm sure, now go into the garden and wait until I'm ready to leave.'

I went out dragging my feet, my hands thrust deep into my pockets. I kicked an imaginary stone in annoyance.

When we arrived at John's I put the hands on the shiny metal coffee table. Our parents talked. When they had finished they turned to us.

'Well?' my mother questioned. With a puzzled frown John said, 'Here you are Rod,' as he handed me a green plastic bag.

'The hands are on the table.'

'Yeah, see you tomorrow, in Wormy's lesson.' We went home.

In my bedroom I turned the plastic bag upside down, but onto the fluffy carpet fell a stone, a tatty note and a pair of gripping hands.

'We sussed em alrite,' was scrawled on the paper . . .

I grinned and began to plan the next battle.

Roderick Harris

The worst kids in the world

The Herdmans were absolutely the worst kids in the history of the world. They lied and stole and smoked cigars (even the girls) and talked dirty and hit little kids and cussed their teachers and took the name of the Lord in vain and set fire to Fred Shoemaker's old broken-down toolhouse.

The toolhouse burned right down to the ground, and I think that surprised the Herdmans. They set fire to things all the time, but that was the first time they managed to burn down a whole building.

I guess it was an accident. I don't suppose they woke up that morning and said to one another, 'Let's go burn down Fred Shoemaker's toolhouse' . . . but maybe they did. After all, it was a Saturday, and not much going on.

It was a terrific fire – two engines and two police cars and all the volunteer firemen and five dozen doughnuts sent up from the Tasti-Lunch Diner. The doughnuts were supposed to be for the firemen, but by the time they got the fire out the doughnuts were all gone. The Herdmans got them – what they couldn't eat they stuffed in their pockets and down the front of their shirts. You could actually *see* the doughnuts all around Ollie Herdman's middle.

I couldn't understand why the Herdmans were hanging around the scene of their crime. Everybody knew the whole thing was their fault, and you'd think they'd have the brains to get out of sight.

One fireman even collared Claude Herdman and said, 'Did you kids start this fire, smoking cigars in that toolhouse?'

But Claude just said, 'We weren't smoking cigars.'

And they weren't. They were playing with Leroy Herdman's 'Young Einstein' chemistry set, which he stole from the hardware store, and that was how they started the fire.

Leroy said so. 'We mixed all the little powders together,' he said, 'and poured lighter fluid around on them and set fire to the lighter fluid. We wanted to see if the chemistry set was any good.'

Any other kid – even a mean kid – would have been a little bit worried if he stole $4.95 worth of something and then burned down a building with it. But Leroy was just mad because the chemistry set got burned up along with everything else before he had a chance to make one or two bombs.

The fire chief got us all together – there were fifteen or twenty kids standing around watching the fire – and gave us a little talk about playing with matches and gasoline and dangerous things like that.

'I don't say that's what happened here,' he told us. 'I don't *know* what happened here, but that could have been it, and you see the result. So let this be a good lesson to you, boys and girls.'

Of course it was a great lesson to the Herdmans – they learned that wherever there's a fire there will be free doughnuts sooner or later.

I guess things would have been different if they'd burned down, say, the Second Presbyterian Church instead of the toolhouse, but the toolhouse was about to fall down anyway. All the neighbours had pestered Mr Shoemaker to do something about it because it looked so awful and was sure to bring rats. So everybody said the fire was a blessing in disguise, and even Mr Shoemaker said it was a relief. My father said it was the only good thing the Herdmans ever did, and if they'd *known* it was a good thing, they wouldn't have done it at all. They would have set fire to something else . . . or somebody.

They were just so all-round awful you could hardly believe they were real: Ralph, Imogene, Leroy, Claude, Ollie, and Gladys – six skinny, stringy-haired kids all alike except for being different sizes and having different black-and-blue places where they had clonked each other.

Barbara Robinson

Anger

the anger was all over my leg
where I was given a kick
I thought the place was burning hot
but all I had was a red patch
the anger filled my heart and my head
I felt the water coming out of my eyes
then all my body was burning like flames
the anger was still in my heart
I thought ,
I shall kick him back
but I knew I hadn't the guts
the water burst from my eyes
like a burst pipe.

Linda Rowe

The cover

'lerrus go mam . . . aw, go on . . . lerrus go, eh, mam?'

We had fled back home from the village shops after following a man walking on tall sticks. He had been pasting up bits of coloured paper to an interested following of small, grubby children just out of school. I had read out the words with my fingers following the lines . . . 'Circus . . . the Big Top . . . Roll up,' to excited youngsters who had skipped after a man calling, 'Hey . . . hey mista, when's the circus then mista?' Then, foiled by his dour silence had skipped back to me as I read on. 'This evenin' for one night on'y . . .' Their mouths made dark 'o's, eyes round and excited.

We had never seen a circus, but my grandad had told me of the time he put his head in a lion's mouth an' it had bit it off so that he had to have it sewn back on again. But then, my grandad wasn't reliable like, he was only telling me that cos I had fell an' grazed my knee an' he was fed up of my yells. I didn't believe they had sewn it back on, cos it would 'ave swallowed it, so there.

'. . . Eh mam, eh . . . can us go mam . . . eh mam, eh?' I paused for breath, 'On'y two an' six mam, an' tha's for grown-ups mam, less for kids . . . can us mam?' Battered down by my harrassment she flapped me away from her skirts. 'Wait an' ask your dad . . .' I kicked at my small sister with my toe, best ger at our mam while she were weakening. My sister opened her mouth as wide as only my sister could. 'Waaahhhh . . . wanna go cer-cus . . . wanna go cer-cus . . . Waaahhhh wanna . . .' Music it were.

'Alright, alright . . . let me think, do!' said my mother with head in hands. 'Where is it? How much is it? An' what time is it?' We blinked at her. 'It's on the waste bit o'land at Pontlottyn mam, shillin' for kids, an' it's this evenin' . . .' I gasped for breath.

'What time does it start child, what time does it start an' end?' I had the poster in my mind's eye and the blasted time evaded me. Well, this evenin' was this evenin' as far as I was concerned.

Grandad walked in and was alarmed and astonished at a set of three voices all talking to him at once.

'Dad, have you heard . . .'

'Grandad, wha' time is . . .'

'Danda . . . take me . . .'

He backed up against the wall with knobbly fingers outstretched. 'Hang on . . .!' he shouted. We were quiet and he turned to our mam for her to explain.

'Ahhh! I saw the posters, right seedy ol' thin's they were too. It starts . . .' He paused to pull at his pipe. 'Grandad!' we yelled, wicked ol' devel grinned. 'Six . . . er no, seven thirty 'til nine of the clock.'

Our eyes swivelled to mam. She sat placid. Bunging mush into the baby's mouth after tasting it first. The baby blew it all out so she had to keep scooping it up an' bunging it back

again . . . fair made yer sick it did.

'. . . I'll tek our Anne mam, ain't gorra cross no roads . . . mam?' She looked speculatingly at grandad, who put on his limp to his chair and sat down mutterin' about his ol' bones. She looked at me. I drew myself up to my nine years of growin' and smiled, remembered my missing front tooth and glowered instead. She sighed heavily.

'Hurray . . . we are goin' the circus . . . we are goin' circus . . .' We danced about her like a pair of crazed loons.

But there's a fly in every ointment, as our mam was apt to say, though goodness knows why.

'Wash . . . change . . . tea . . .' she bellowed, 'Wash your sister, change her knickers an' socks while I get your tea.' She plonked the baby to dribble drunkenly on to grandad. I sighed.

With dire warnings still ringing in my ears I held Anne's paw in one hand an' the money in the other. Approaching the waste land off Pontlottyn, there were lights everywhere in a circle . . . Beyond that circle was a fearsome darkness. Anne clung tightly to me. 'Don't like it . . .' she muttered. 'Yer 'aven't see'd it yet . . . so 'ow do you know dumbo?' I answered. But I was feeling a bit like not liking it myself. I could hear no lions roaring, no elephants trumpeting . . . just mad ol' dogs chained up to the dirty caravans and foaming at the mouth to get at us . . . the mud was nearly up to our knees . . . so much for our washes. I had known at the time it had been a waste of water.

'Well . . . you comin' or not?' A fat, bulging lady wearing lots of red paint on her face snatched the money from my fist with red talons like a witch's. I jumped and gathered up the two cloakroom tickets, we stumbled through the filthy mud. I lifted Anne to my hip where her wellies dribbled muddy drool down my clean dress. The dogs renewed their frenzied assaults . . . 'Sod off . . .!' she yelled. (Where had she learned those words? I stored them for future use . . .) We reached a tent and a hand came out of the darkness and grabbed at us, shoving us to rickety chairs on which planks were laid . . . we sat on the edge of one end and the other side shot up in the air until it was anchored by a sweating man who shoved someone to sit on that end. Then the chair collapsed and my bottom was uncomfortable with thick, gooey, black mud.

Finally we were all sat down with bright, expectant eyes fixed on sounds coming from behind various openings in the canvas. Sounds that sounded very much like the words grandad used to mutter when my dad went on at him.

There was butcher's sawdust on the floor in a circle, an' walked-in dog an' pony muck. The tent was filling up and talking grew to a loud buzz.

'W'en we gonna start?' asked Anne.

'Soon . . .' I muttered.

'Wanna hot-dawg,' she said loudly.

'I ain't gor no money,' I muttered, my face turning red.

'Wanna hot da-wg, wanna hot da-wg, wanna . . . ' She began to bellow as only my sister could. A filthy boy shoved a greasy roll under her nose.

' 'Ow much?' I asked in a loud whisper. With gritted teeth.

' 'Ow much yer gor?' he snarled at me. I counted slowly.

'Sixpence.' I said.

'Then they're sixpence,' he growled. I shoved it half-way down Anne's throat. 'Now will yer shuddup!' I said.

The canvas bulged out in several places, then a man dressed in red with a tall black hat staggered out, slid in the dog muck an' by twisting his body kept his balance. He stood swaying with great intakes of breath. A silence fell. 'Laydees an' gent-el-men an' child-eren . . . may I . . . (hic) presen' the (hic) CURCUSSS . . .' He stumbled back to a few half-hearted handclaps.

Anne had her mouth stuffed bulging with roll an' onions, no sign of a sausage. She searched about her, then gave up, her mouth too full to argue or complain.

Two little black ponies bolted in as if shot from a cannon. They saw the rows of people an' their legs went backwards like frantic to get away. A whip cracked, they froze then, one limping badly with a swollen hock, went through a crazy

78

dance routine, turning and bowing, red feathers bobbing sadly. Then they bolted back out. The audience clapped in sympathy.

The man in the red an' black outfit was back. 'Naww . . . may I (hic) present Madame (hic) an' her fam-us dogs . . .'

Five mangy little poodles ran about the ring, messing it up some more and scratching at naked pink patches on their coats. Anne stopped chewing, remembering the bared teeth of the chained dogs outside. She moved closer to me and the plank clonked up at the other end, dropping a neatly-dressed man into the mud. I clouted her absent-mindedly as I watched the neat man trying to scrape gunge off his best pin-stripes. I frowned at her, trying not to laugh. The lady with the tickets at the door was in the ring with no dress on. She had red stockin's an' a silver swimsuit pinned up under one arm with a big safety pin. She carried hoops. The little dogs in gold tassles ran round an' round sometimes duckin' under the hoop an' sometimes jumping over when she tripped them up with it.
[. . .]
Some big boys in the front began to slow hand-clap an' chant. 'Wher's the li-ons, wher's the li-ons, wher's the lions.' A man with baggy red trousers stumbled out, he had balloons tied to a broken bowler hat and a sad face painted on. He tipped over buckets of water, threw sawdust over the neat man an' made a right ol' fool of hisself.

The roof leaked down our necks and we were shivering with cold and excitement, though the excitement was being replaced with revulsion and disgust. Hardened ol' farmers there with their families muttered loudly about the state of the animals. A spangled, little dwarf joined the first clown and the antics grew wilder to drown out the sound of jeers and slow hand-claps. Anne was choking on the dry roll. I bashed her on the back until she had coughed it up. Tears were streaming down her grubby face.

'Don' like no cer-cus,' she sobbed sadly. Me neither!

The two clowns were fixing up a rope between two posts, with a ladder goin' up. Anne stared. The swaying man came on still in his top-hat but with no trousers. In red stockin's an' silver swimsuit he tried to climb the ladder. He would get one foot on, then the other would slip. Loud guffaws came from the restless crowd. With drunken dignity he made it to the top of the pole and sat there hanging on. Sweat ran down his face and his grease-paint melted. There was a silence to chew on. Slowly he stood . . . a drum-roll just about knocked him off balance but he sweated some more, ran half-way across the bending rope, an' fell off. The silence grew to a strain. After his third tumble, Anne opened her mouth to its widest, with greasy strands of onions running down her chin she bellowed, 'Waaahhhh . . . don' like no cer-cus, don' like no cer-cus . . . Waaaahhhh . . . ahh . . .' Everyone clapped and cheered. She stopped crying immediately and dimpled her sweetest smile. I sank into my collar. 'I'll kill yer. I will too, yer little cow!'

The ring was suddenly full of all the circus acts together, but it was hard to compete with my bitch-sister's four-year-old lungs. Between the gasps for breath she smiled for the approval of the audience. People stood, gathering belongings, children, balloons . . . all covered in thick, black mud. I dragged Anne to the flap that was a door. I'd swing for her I would an' all.

'Wanna see th' lions,' she muttered.

'There ain't no lions,' I said through clenched teeth.

'Wanna see elefan's.'

'There ain't no elephants.'

'Wanna see . . .'

'SOD OFF!' I yelled the word that she had taught me earlier. She stood in the mud, gaping at me, looking like a lost an' found stray. Urgggghh! I hated her I did. I glared at her. 'Oooh, you just wait 'til I see your mam!' said a familiar voice. The woman's lips were pursed with disapproval. I wanted to weep. Grandad had said there would be lions, an' tigers, an' elephants . . . our dog cudda done better. Our grandad was gonna cop it when I saw our grandad an' all. It wasn't fair. The dogs chained to the peeling caravans snarled and tried to bite our legs as we stumbled past.

'Dear God Almighty . . . did you CRAWL home?' asked my mam, in a whisper not to wake the baby. We trailed·mud over her clean floors. I snuffled. Anne glowered darkly.

'Don' like no cer-cusss,' she said, like a dog with an' ol' bone. I sniffed louder. Mum took no notice. She held paper. 'Get them boots off quick, here . . . tread on this newspaper.' She was frantically laying newspaper over the floor . . . too late, Anne was sick. Right in the middle of our only good rug. Onions floated in green bile. It looked revolting.

'God forbid. What have you been giving that poor child?' The 'poor child' looked sickly smugger. I flung my boots onto the floor.

'I 'ates that kid, I 'ates circuses, I 'ates everything,' I screamed brokenly. Grandad shuffled in wearing his worn-out slippers. 'An' I 'ates you too!' I yelled to his astonished face. I threw rather a good, effective tantrum.

Grandad cleaned up the sick and the mud. Mam plonked us both into a hot, soapy bath. With Dettol. I sat amidst the multicoloured bubbles and thought about circuses.

'Ma-aam,' I cried, and she snatched up a bowl, just in time for me to be heavenly sick.

The next day it was a Saturday. I wandered about the site of the circus, all the messed up ground with its litter and drying mud. There were police everywhere, taking notes in little black books.

I legged it home and got in just in time to hear my dad say, 'Did it while everybody was at that circus. Perfect time see? Others went out and just broke into the houses and cleaned them out. That darn circus was just a cover see? But . . . Glamorgan police are on to them. Oh yes . . . won't get away from us I can tell you.' And he hooked his thumbs into the breast pockets of his uniform and looked as smug as only my dad could, when he was winning. He winked at me, grinning.

'Circuses . . .' he sneered.

Joan M. Batchelor

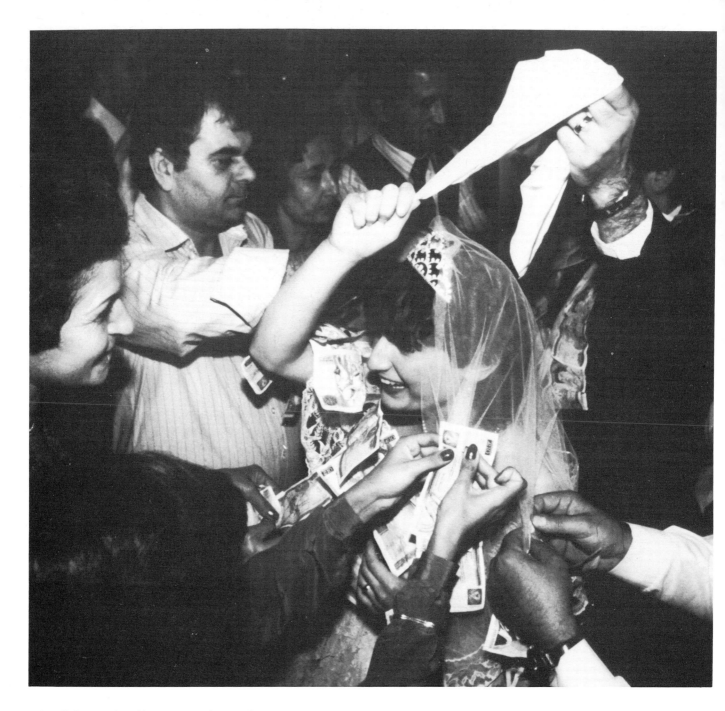

Wedding bells: Greek style

The large hall buzzed with excitement: tables were grouped close together, people's bodies bulging over the edges. Every available inch was crammed with bodies, their legs together, arms by their sides and still taking up each other's space. Paper plates filled with food were stacked on top of one another on the tables; half-filled bottles of Scotch, wine and ouzo also cluttered their surfaces. Bread was piled high in the middle and the people were consuming it with unbelievable avidity, dipping it into the thick, white bread-dip dotted with chunks of garlic.

The round tables were set at the edge of the spacious dance-floor, which remained empty while the people were eating with unabated vigour. They spoke and ate at the same time, arms waving about, illustrating their conversation. Small children ran around the tables, weaving between the table-legs and the flailing arms. They ran shrieking, collecting the tops from the tins to make necklaces, bracelets or whatever they happened to fancy. Mothers chased them, shrilling in their fast Greek dialects. As the children, resentful at their

interrupted bliss, refused to go back to their tables, their mothers dragged them by the hair, blood-vessels bursting and eyes blazing.

Then the band began to play and the hall was filled with the melodious chords and arpeggios of the bouzouki. Several men and women stood up to dance. Arms outstretched, heads up, they picked up the rhythm of the music. They danced till the globules of sweat stood out on their foreheads. At last came the time for the traditional dance of the bride and groom.

Gracefully the bride rose and walked beside her husband to the centre of the floor. As the couple, with a handkerchief held between them, danced, one by one people came and pinned money on them. Husbands stopped drinking and wives forgot about their children, for this was the climax of the wedding. Photograph-bulbs flashed, and the couple smiled their thanks sweetly and kissed the cheeks of the donors.

Angela Joannou

Drummers at a funeral dance, Nigeria.

The funeral dance

Death is a very important event in any family and is usually marked by ceremonies of various kinds. In the passage that follows, Peter Obiese, a journalist, who is spending his leave in his home village, is taken to see the funeral dance for a local man; the dance is performed by young girls, and his sister-in-law, who accompanies him, hopes that he will be attracted by one of the dancers who has been singled out to be a suitable wife for him.

Music, mingled with rounds of applause, grew louder as we advanced towards Ota village square where the funeral dance was taking place. There were two dance clubs, each surrounded by a crowd of spectators. One was from the deceased's own village, and the other from his mother's village.

We picked our way through the crowd, first to one club and then to the other. This last club was the one from Nneka's village. We found a convenient spot from where we could see the dancers with very little chance of their seeing us.

Girls in every village formed themselves into an *egwu aja* dance club. Membership was open to all girls in the village. Except at funerals their dance was rarely done after its premiere showing. The deceased's mother had come from the same village as Nneka and Bessie; that was why their village girls' dance club was in attendance. Membership of the club ceased at marriage.

Like every *egwu aja* dance club, this one had learnt a variety of dances. Groups of eight or more girls were called upon to dance at the same time. The small ones opened the show and the oldest and biggest girls danced last. They danced round in a circle, sometimes round the man who supervised them at practices and at public shows. When each group of dancers had done two or three numbers, it retired and another group took its place.

There were over forty members of the dance club present. They stood together, occupying about one-third of the circular space which the crowd had allowed them. They all wore blouses of the same material. This was all that was uniform about their dress. Their loin cloths varied. Those who could afford bells had rows of them circling their waists. They each had a pair of clappers which resembled butter-pats. Three of the girls carried clay pots on their laps. Each pot had two holes, one on the top and one on its side. With these clappers and clay pots they beat time for the dancers.

There was still confusion in the centre of the circle as we took our places among the watching spectators. A group had just finished dancing and spectators were walking in and out among them, making presents to their relatives, their friends and the best performers in the group. The space gradually became clearer and the people quietened down considerably. As we watched, another group took the place of the outgoing one. There were only six girls, including Nneka, in this group, and they were the biggest.

'This is one of the reasons why Nneka is very popular among us,' Bessie told me. 'Most of the girls are school children. Nneka is the only "Miss" among them. She takes her full part in village life and gains a lot of experience by doing so. Many young men go to seek her hand in marriage, but they never succeed. That is because they are either related to her family, her family does not approve of the boys' families, or the boys are poor wretches who are only interested in what they could get from her in the way of dowry. She, however, believes, as you do, that people should marry for love.'

As Bessie spoke, the soloist began singing the few desultory notes which introduced the number they were going to dance. Nneka and her companions arranged themselves in a circle and stood listening to her. The soloist sang and stopped and sang again. She was a good soloist by our standards. Her voice was as sweet and as clear as that of a partridge. She had left out the original wording of the song and was improvising as she went on. Sometimes she sang in praise of the dancers, sometimes in praise of the spectators, and sometimes in praise of the dead whom they had come to honour. Then she cleverly went back to the original wording. The music strengthened into a well-timed song.

The girls took up the chorus, which they sang in unison, breaking into harmony when and where the fancy took them. They began to beat their clappers and pots and Nneka and her companions began to move. At first they moved slowly, but as the tempo quickened and they caught the spirit of the dance, the pace increased.

They leaped up and down. They bent and stretched themselves, straining every muscle. They turned this way and that and occasionally round about. They all moved together as one girl, performing the same motions as if without thought. They performed easy as well as difficult steps, their feet tracing intricate patterns on the dusty ground. They danced well. They danced to impress the male spectators who were very critical of dances by girls and women. They danced to impress those who had come to this selection ground, each to find for himself a wife. They danced for the prestige and honour of their village. And they danced for the joy of dancing. It was evident from the smiles that hovered round the lips that they were enjoying every minute of it, despite the strenuous effort which their dancing called for.

Perhaps because I had gone particularly to see Nneka, I thought she was the best dancer of the lot. Her movements were graceful and, at intervals, she introduced some movements peculiar to herself, which distinguished her from the remaining five. I looked on enchanted. Occasionally the soloist called one of the dancing girls by name and reminded her, in song, what an excellent dancer her mother was. This was intended to bring out the best in the girl thus addressed. When this happened she yelled in delight and did some little figure, all on her own, which sent the crowd applauding. Yet none of these flourishes, to me, beat what Nneka could do. Once, when she was called endearing names by the soloist, she stood on her toes, gesticulating, her whole frame quivering. The crowd had responded by throwing coins at her feet. It was unbeatable!

They only did one number and stopped, for it was almost time to bury the deceased. The crowd could not contain itself when the dance was over. It broke into a frenzy and spread all over the whole place. For about ten minutes Bessie and I could not make out Nneka in the crowd. At last we saw her, cornered by three elderly women who were praising her efforts.

Onuora Nzekwu

82

Bonfire night and Mr Ellison

On the bombed side of the street,
before they plonked those shoe-box prefabs down,
we raised our bonfire, roofing it
with planks we'd nicked from Barney's Yard.
And when night came and we were still
awake in all its wickedness,
we prodded rolled newspaper torches
between the planks to let the fire rip.

But in the awe of it, the hush,
we heard the Elloe's drunken father curse
and clatter like a one-man-band
along the street. And next,
the pistol shot of a slammed front door,
his whingeing wife,
thin as a needle, quick as a pain,
dragging off four yapping dogs of sons
around the foundry corner
and away up Knowsley Road.

No one called me in. I was left
with a bonfire playing merry hell
with the dark, while half-seas Mr Ellison,
tottering like a bull come round
from surgery, hauled out and flung
curtains, chairs, and table legs
among the splintering flames. And moved
by generosity: 'There's something
for your bommy, Matt.'

Finally the sideboard's bulk.
But halfway across the cobbled street
strength and fury failed. 'I'll have
a bloody bommy by meself,' he said,
striking matches into drawers.

Just two of us, alone, with darkness winning:
me not twelve years old, and him
slumped on the kerbstones, blubbering.

Matt Simpson

November 5th

November the fifth has come and gone,
But thoughts of it still linger,
I held a banger in my hand,
Has anyone seen my finger?

Sharon O'Sullivan

Happy Christmas

It was a boring Christmas this year.
My dad went out, had six pints,
Got drunk, started singing,
And kicked the cat.

It was a boring Christmas this year.
I got a game called 'Maniac'.
(Do you think they're trying to tell me something?)
My brother got a shining rocking horse
But of course . . . only wanted the box.

It was a boring Christmas this year.
Dinner was followed by a full-scale argument.
I sat there with a mouthful of turkey
Listening to the commotion,
While my brother spat peas at the injured cat.

It was a boring Christmas this year.
My dad tripped over the table-tennis bat,
Told me to put my noisy toy away,
Said he was changing it for something quiet.

(Anon.)

Albert and the liner

Below the military striking clock in the City Arcade there was, and for all I know still is, a fabulous toyshop.

It was a magic grotto, that shop. A zoo, a circus, a pantomime, a travelling show, a railway exhibition, an enchanted public library, a clockwork museum, an archive of boxed games, a pavilion of sports equipment, a depository of all the joys of the indefinite, endless leisure of the winter holiday – but first, the military striking clock.

Once a year we were taken to see the clock strike noon – an event in our lives as colourful, and traditional, and as fixed and immovable in the calendar of pageantry as Trooping the Colour. Everybody who was anybody assembled, a few minutes before twelve, on the patch of worn tiles incorporating an advertisement for tomato sausages done in tasteful mosaic, beneath that military striking clock.

There was me, and Jack Corrigan, and the crippled lad from No. 43, and there was even Albert Skinner – whose father never took him anywhere, not even to the Education Office to explain why he'd been playing truant.

Albert Skinner, with his shaved head and his shirt-lap hanging out of his trousers, somehow attached himself, insinuated himself, like a stray dog. You'd be waiting at the tram stop with your mother, all dolled up in your Sunday clothes for going into town and witnessing the ceremony of the military striking clock, and Albert, suddenly, out of nowhere, would be among those present.

'Nah, then, kid.'

And your mother, out of curiosity, would say – as she was meant to say – 'You're never going into town looking like that, are you, Albert?'

And Albert would say: 'No. I was, only I've lost my tram fare.'

And your mother, out of pity, would say – as she was meant to say – 'Well, you can come with us. But you'll have to tidy yourself up. Tuck your shirt in, Albert.'

So at Christmastime Albert tagged on to see the military striking clock strike noon. And after the mechanical soldiers of the King had trundled back into their plaster-of-Paris garrison, he, with the rest of us, was allowed to press his nose to the fabulous toyshop window.

Following a suitable period of meditation, we were then treated to a bag of mint imperials – '*and think on, they're to share between you*' – and conveyed home on the rattling tram. And there, thawing out our mottled legs by the fireside, we were supposed to compose our petitions to Father Christmas.

Dear Father Christmas, for Christmas I would like . . .

'Don't know what to put,' we'd say at length to one another, seeking some kind of corporate inspiration.

'Why don't you ask him for a sledge? I am.'

'Barmpot, what do you want a sledge for? What if it doesn't snow?'

'Well – a cricket bat and stumps, and that.'

'Don't play cricket at Christmas, barmpot.'

Albert Skinner said nothing. Nobody, in fact, said anything worth saying, during those tortured hours of voluntary composition.

With our blank jumbo jotters on our knees, we would suck our copying-ink pencils until our tongues turned purple – but it wasn't that we were short of ideas. Far from it: sledges, cricket bats with stumps and that, fountain pens, dynamos, cinematographs complete with Mickey Mouse films – the fact of the matter was, there was too much choice.

For the fabulous toyshop, which sparked off our exotic and finally blank imaginations, was the nearest thing on this earth to Santa's Workshop. It was like a bankruptcy sale in heaven. The big clockwork train ran clockwise and the small electric train ran anti-clockwise, and there was Noah's Ark, and a tram conductor's set, and a junior typewriter revolving on a brightly-lit glass shelf, and a fairy cycle hanging from the ceiling on invisible wires, and a tin steam roller, and the Tip-Top Annual and the Film Fun Annual and the Radio Fun Annual and the Jingles Annual and the Joker Annual and the Jester Annual, and board games, and chemistry sets, and conjuring sets, and carpentry sets – everything, in short, that the modern boy would give his eye-teeth for.

Everything that Albert Skinner would have given his eye-teeth for, in fact, and much that Albert Skinner would never get. And not only him. There were items that no reasonable modern boy expected to find in his Christmas pillow-case – not even though he bartered every tooth in his head and promised to be a good lad till kingdom come.

The centrepiece of the fabulous toyshop's window display was always something out of reach of ordinary mortals, such as the Blackpool Tower in Meccano, or a mechanical carousel with horses that went up and down on their brass poles like the real thing, or Windsor Castle made of a million building bricks, or Buckingham Palace with nobs on – floodlit. None of us had to be told that such luxuries were beyond Father Christmas's price range.

This year the window featured a splendid model of the *Queen Mary*, which had recently been launched on Clydebank. It was about four feet long, with real lights in the portholes, real steam curling out of the funnels, and a crew, and passengers, and lifeboats, and cabin trunks, all to scale – and clearly it was not for the likes of us.

Having seen it and marvelled at it, we dismissed this expensive dream from our minds, sucked our copying-ink pencils and settled down to list our prosaic requests – for Plasticine, for farmyard animals that poisoned you when you licked the paint off, and for one pair of roller skates between two of us.

All of us, that is to say, except Albert Skinner. Having considered several possibilities, and taken advice on the rival merits of a racing track with eight electric sports cars and a glove puppet of Felix the Cat he'd rather fancied, Albert calmly announced that he'd given thought to all our suggestions and he was asking Father Christmas for the *Queen Mary*.

*The Cunard White Star liner **Queen Mary** leaving Southampton on her maiden voyage to New York in 1936.*

This, as you might imagine, was greeted with some scepticism.

'What – that one in the Arcade window? With all the lights and the steam coming out and that? You've never asked for that, have you?'

'Yeh – course I have. Why shouldn't I?'

'He's blinking crackers. Hey, Skinno, why don't you ask for them soldiers that march in and out and bang the clock? Because you've more chance of getting them than that *Queen Mary*.'

'If I'd wanted them soldiers I'd have asked for them. Only I don't. So I've asked him for the *Queen Mary*.'

'Who – Father Christmas?'

'No – him on the Quaker Oats Box, who do you think?'

'Bet you haven't, man. Bet you're having us on.'

'I'm not – God's honour. I've asked him for the *Queen Mary*.'

'Let's see the letter, then.'

'Can't – I've chucked it up the chimney.'

'Yeh – bet you have. Anyway, your dad won't get it for you – he can't afford it.'

'What's it got to do with him? I'm asking Father Stinking Rotten Christmas for it, not me dad. Dozy.'

'What else have you asked for, Skinno?'

'Nowt. I don't want owt else. I just want the *Queen Mary*. And I'm getting it, as well.'

Little else was said at the time, but privately we thought Albert was a bit of an optimist. For one thing, the *Queen Mary* was so big and so grand and so lit-up that it was probably not even for sale. For another, we were all well aware that Father Christmas's representative in the Skinner household was a sullen, foul-tempered collier who also happened to be unemployed.

Albert's birthday present, it was generally known, had been a pair of boots – instead of the scooter on which, at that time, he had set his heart.

Even so, Albert continued to insist that he was getting the *Queen Mary* for Christmas. 'Ask my dad,' he would say. 'If you don't believe me, ask my dad.'

None of us cared to broach the subject with the excitable Mr Skinner. But sometimes, when we went to his house to swop comics, Albert would raise the matter himself.

'Dad, I am aren't I? Aren't I, Dad? Getting that *Queen Mary* for Christmas?'

Mr Skinner, dourly whittling a piece of wood by the fireside after the habit of all the local miners, would growl without looking up: 'You'll get a clout over the bloody earhole if you don't stop chelping.'

Albert would turn complacently to us. 'I am, see. I'm getting the *Queen Mary*. Aren't I Dad? Dad? Aren't I?'

Sometimes when his father had come home from the pub in

a bad mood (which was quite often), Albert's pleas for reassurance would be met with a more vicious response. 'Will you shut up about the bloody Queen swining Mary!' Mr Skinner would shout. 'You gormless little git, do you think I'm made of money?'

Outside, his ear tingling from the blow his father had landed on it, Albert would bite back the tears and declare stubbornly: 'I'm still getting it. You wait till Christmas.'

Christmas Eve was but a fortnight off by then. Most of us had a shrewd idea, from hints dropped by our mothers, what Father Christmas would be bringing us – or, in most cases, not bringing. 'I don't think Father Christmas can manage an electric train set this year, our Terry. He says they're too expensive. He says he might be able to find you a tip-up lorry.'

Being realists, we accepted our lowly position on Father Christmas's scale of priorities – and we tried our best to persuade Albert to accept his.

'You're not *forced* to get that *Queen Mary*, you know, Skinno.'

'Who says I'm not?'

'My mam. She says it's too big to go in Father Christmas's sack.'

'Yeh, well that's all *she* knows. Because he's fetching Jacky Corrigan a fairy cycle – so if he can't get the *Queen Mary* in his sack, how can he get a stinking rotten fairy cycle?'

'Yeh, well he isn't fetching me a fairy cycle at all, cleverclogs, he's fetching me a John Bull printing outfit. 'Cos he told my mam.'

'I don't care what he told her, or what he didn't tell her. He's still fetching me that *Queen Mary*.'

The discussion was broken up by the sudden appearance of Mr Skinner at their scullery window. 'If I hear one more bloody word from you about that bloody *Queen Mary*, you'll get nothing for Christmas! Do you hear me?' And there the matter rested.

A few days later the crippled lad at No. 43 was taken by the Church Ladies Guild to see the military striking clock in the City Arcade, and when he came home he reported that the model of the *Queen Mary* was no longer in the window of the fabulous toyshop.

'I know,' said Albert, having confirmed that his father was out of earshot. 'I'm getting it for Christmas.'

And indeed, it seemed the only explanation possible. The fabulous toyshop never changed its glittering display until after Boxing Day – it was unheard of. Some minor item might vanish out of the window – the Noah's Ark, perhaps, or a farmyard, or a game of Monopoly or two. There was a rational explanation for this: Father Christmas hadn't enough toys to go round and he'd been obliged, so to speak, to call on his sub-contractors. But the set-piece, the Blackpool Tower made out of Meccano or the carousel with the horses that went round and round and up and down – that was never removed; never. And yet the *Queen Mary* had gone. What had happened? Had Father Christmas gone mad? Had Mr Skinner bribed him – and if so, with what? Had Mr Skinner won the football pools? Or was it that Albert's unswerving faith could move mountains – not to mention ocean-going liners with real steam and real lights in the portholes? Or was it, as one cynic among us insisted, that the *Queen Mary* had been privately purchased for some pampered grammar school lad on the posher side of town?

'You just wait and see,' said Albert.

And then it was Christmas morning; and after the chocolate pennies had been eaten and all the kitchens in the street were awash with nut-shells and orange peel, we all flocked out to show off our presents – sucking our brand-new torches to make our cheeks glow red, or brandishing a lead soldier or two in the pretence that we had a whole regiment of them indoors. Those who had wanted wooden forts were delighted with their painting books; those who had prayed for electric racing cars were content with their Dinky toys; those who had asked for roller skates were happy with their pencil boxes; and there was no sign of Albert.

No one, in fact, expected to see him at all. But just as we were asking each other what Father Christmas could have brought him – a new jersey, perhaps, or a balaclava helmet – he came bounding, leaping, jumping, almost somersaulting into the street. 'I've got it! I've got it! I've got it!'

Painting books and marbles and games of Happy Families were abandoned in the gutter as we clustered around Albert, who was cradling in his arms what seemed on first inspection to be a length of wood. Then we saw that it had been roughly carved at both ends, to make a bow and stern, and that three cotton-reels had been nailed to it for funnels. A row of tin-tacks marked the Plimsoll line, and there were stuck-on bits of cardboard for the portholes. The whole thing was painted over in sticky lamp-black, except for the lettering on the portside.

'*The Queen Mary*,' it said. In white, wobbling letters. Capital T, small h, capital E. Capital Q, small u, capital E, capital E, small n. Capital M, small a, capital R, small y. Penmanship had never been Mr Skinner's strong point.

'See!' crowed Albert complacently. 'I told you he'd fetch me it, and he's fetched me it.'

Our grunts of appreciation, though somewhat strained, were genuine enough. Albert's *Queen Mary* was a crude piece of work, but clearly many hours of labour, and much love, had gone into it. Its clumsy contours alone must have taken night after night of whittling by the fireside.

Mr Skinner, pyjama-jacket tucked into his trousers, had come out of the house and was standing by his garden gate. Albert, in a rush of happiness, ran to his father and flung his arms around him and hugged him. Then he waved the *Queen Mary* on high.

'Look, Dad! Look what I've got for Christmas! Look what Father Christmas has fetched me! You knew he would, didn't you, all this time!'

'Get out of it, you soft little bugger,' said Mr Skinner. He drew contentedly on his empty pipe, cuffed Albert over the head as a matter of habit, and went indoors.

Keith Waterhouse

Breadcrumb's birthday

Leslie Thomas spent part of his childhood in a children's home – Dr Barnardo's – which the boys called 'Dickies'. There he met George, nicknamed Breadcrumb because of his habit of scooping up and eating all the breadcrumbs from the dinner table.

Marlow had been invalided out of the RAF and had returned to Dickies as the Gaffer's only assistant. He was a shortish, good-looking man, who had achieved the near-impossible of being wholly popular with the boys and being strong enough to demand respect at the same time.

He could talk with you on equal terms, tell good yarns, and yet never be held in the contempt that familiarity so often induces. When he lost his temper it was best to clear out. Anywhere.

There came a morning when Breadcrumb George sat up in bed and announced that it was his birthday. He was one of those who had never received a letter or a parcel from anyone in all his life. But that day one of the kids stopped him and said: 'Breadcrumb, there's a parcel for you in the Gaffer's office.'

Breadcrumb whooped a foot into the air and tore around, crazily, almost incoherently happy, shouting 'Guess what – I've got a parcel! I've got a parcel!'

He couldn't make a guess about who had sent the gift. But it was there. Plenty of the boys had seen it. About lunchtime the parcel appeared on his bed. He went into the dormitory and it sat there waiting for him, like a reward for goodness, beautifully tied, stamped and addressed.

Almost dumb with wonder and happiness he picked it up and examined it. Then he tugged and tore away the string and pulled the paper apart. Out on to his bed and the floor shot an avalanche of breadcrumbs.

With the infinite cruelty that only children can inflict on other children the trick had been planned, the bait laid, and the trap sprung. Breadcrumb George sat there crying salt tears, with the crumbs all around him.

Marlow walked in. Breadcrumb was a tough character and he was no great friend of Marlow's. But the master realised what had been done in the time it took him to stride from the door. Never had he been so angry. He howled around, blistering to get his hands on the guilty boys. No one told, so he cancelled the swimming for that day. Then he told Breadcrumb to get cleaned up and in his best clothes, he collected money from everyone on the staff, bullying it out of half of them, and took Breadcrumb into King's Lynn.

Breadcrumb crept into the dormitory late that night. He had a parcel under his arm containing a real present. He put it down on his locker, undressed and got into bed.

'What was it like, Breadcrumb?' came a muted voice from half-way under a blanket.

'Went to the pictures,' announced Breadcrumb. 'Got a new pair of togger boots and my guts full of cream buns. It was all right.'

Leslie Thomas

The budgie's New Year message

Get a little tin of bird-seed,
Pour it in my little trough.
If you don't, you little twit, I'll
Bite your little finger off!

Kit Wright

Dinner party blues

I eat

Children's food
and I hate it
You know the old rubbish I mean
dead worms in red puke called spaghetti
and always the good old baked beans

My parents are giving a party tonight
Just a few people coming to 'dine'
And everyone's stomach gets filled with delights
With just one exception – that's mine

I got

Children's food
and I hate it
two hours before they arrived
not cheese but
wet rubber all wrapped up in foil
and toast that was burnt on both sides

At six-thirty tonight I was tortured
Though Mum never noticed my plight
When I sat in the kitchen and ate my baked beans
While she cooked a roast duck for tonight

I had

Children's food
and I hate it
beefburgers instead of real meat
and never whole fish
just the fingers
all the bits that the grown ups won't eat

Oh why can't they feed us like adults
Oh why can't I stay up till late
And eat all the things I can smell here upstairs
Instead of the kid's stuff I hate

But it's

Children's food
and I loathe it
You know the old rubbish I mean
it's anything frozen or
out of a tin
or anything served with baked beans

Mick Gowar

The weekly experience

Watch those tins!
And mind these cans!
Leave the biscuits –
These are that man's.
I don't want that cream
So please put it back,
No, not there –
On the first rack.
Now fetch me the butter
Out of the fridge,
Don't lean over too far,
Stay near the edge.
You can't have the ice-cream,
Leave it alone!
Pass me the lard,
We've got to get home.
Sit in this trolley
Where you'll be out of trouble,
Keep your fingers inside
And don't meddle.
You can't have chocolate
Or sponge cake so thick,
If you eat any more
You're going to be sick.
Now go to the desk,
I'm ready to pay,
Give me the stamps,
Come on, straightaway.
It's always the same
When I bring you, my lad.
Next time I come shopping
I'll leave you with Dad!

Karen Skeldon

Look

Look – said the boy
the scaffold-man at work
is like a spider on his net

No – said the scaffold-man
I'm just a fly
in the trap the spider set

Michael Rosen

Any Saturday in 1920 ✓

Saturday was the happiest day of our life because we got our Saturday penny and our favourite dinner, which was fish and chips.

Now we had to earn this penny. In the first place we had to behave ourselves for a week and in the second place we all had our various jobs to do, Saturday morning, very quietly, because Dad was a London taxi driver and he worked at night and slept during the day. So all our jobs had to be done on tip-toe.

The family consisted of six of us kids – I was the eldest. I was 13 and my own mother had died when I was 7. So after the Great War my Dad remarried. He remarried a war widow. She had four children who were my step-brothers and step-sisters as I had no brother or sister of my own. I was the eldest, 13; then came my step-brother Charlie, 11; then came my step-sister Winnie, 9; my step-brother Jackie, 7; my step-sister Phyllis, who was partially paralysed and had epileptic fits, 5; and a new baby half-brother, Jimmy, who belonged to my Dad, so that we both had the same Dad. He was my nearest blood relation.

The only one that didn't have to do any work was Phil because she could not in those days. So Phyllis used to have to mind Jimmy, because Jimmy was almost blind and, but for the care of Moorfields Hospital and the District Nurse that came in daily, he would have been blind. But owing to their skill and kindness, he overcame this disability. He was not allowed to cry because of his eyes, so one or other of us kids had him in our arms all day. In the first place he wasn't allowed to cry and in the second place, my Dad was sleeping because he worked all night.

My Dad was a huge man. He weighed 17½ stone of muscle and in his younger days had been a amateur wrestling instructor. But he was what I call a gentle giant. He never smacked one of us kids once although he could have snapped us over his knee. He used to shout and could he swear! But he never hit us.

So Saturday morning arrives. Now, if you've ever seen a tin of sardines you'll know how we slept: three girls at the top, two boys at the bottom, the baby in a drawer in Mum's room with Mum and Dad. We only had two rooms and a very tiny kitchen, so as you can imagine, when we got our Dad in there weighing 17½ stones there wasn't any room for anybody or anything else.In any case there was only room for a large table and two chairs. We got up early Saturday because if you got your jobs done in time you had your penny and you went to the Penny Rush. The Penny Rush was the pictures. We used to see a film and a serial with Pearl White in it every week – that is if we got our jobs done in time.

When you went to the cinema, which was called the Central Hall, you had either an orange, a bag of sweets or a pencil given to you; but if you made a row when you got inside you got a clump round the earhole and were slung out! Needless to say, being the eldest I rarely went because I had too many jobs to do, but we used to send Jackie so he could take Jimmy in his arms and we could get rid of at least one noise.

My job was the outside lavatory, which was shared by us

six kids, Mum and Dad and the family of five upstairs. It was my job to clean it, scrub the wooden top, whitewash the sides and scrub the floor. While I was doing this, Jackie, as there was no toilet roll in those days, was tearing up the newspapers for the week making a hole in the corner, and putting the string through to tie the newspaper up in the lavatory in place of a toilet roll. As my Dad was a great gambler – he gambled every day of his life except Sunday – there was a lot of newspapers: he bought all the newspapers under the sun. So there was always a ton of 'bum paper', as we called it. And God help Jackie if the bum paper ran out.

In our yard my Dad kept a goat, a nanny goat, who at the time was pregnant. He thought us kids would drink the milk. He also kept chickens and bred greyhounds. Nanny had two kids. My Dad was midwife. He came rushing in when the first one was born, which was fawn, and rushing in again after the second one was born, which was black and white. Us kids would not drink the milk, although Dad was the milkmaid. He looked charming sitting out there in the yard. All the neighbours used to get on their walls to look at him. None of us kids would drink the milk because it was a dark yellow and we were used to skimmed milk. Dad called us every name you could think of, but I noticed he never drank it himself. But the man next door, named Mr Ryde, who was dying from what in those days we called consumption, drank quite a lot of it, so it didn't all go to waste.

After Jackie's done his bum paper he takes Jimmy to the pictures. He's got his Saturday penny. Winnie has the knives and forks to clean – there was nothing stainless in those days. The forks and the spoons were cleaned with a metal polish which was called 'Bluebell' and the knives were cleaned on a knife board with some stuff that was called 'Monkey Brand'. It cost a penny and lasted almost a year – and God help you if you didn't make it last a year. Anyway, that was Winnie's job. Charlie had all the greengrocery to get because he was a big boy for his age. He was 11 and he had the greengrocery to get and the chicken house to clean out, which was cleaned out once a week. He was not allowed to touch the greyhounds, as they were my father's pride and joy. He thought more of the greyhounds than he did of us kids. Charlie also had to clean Nanny out – and Nanny stank like hell, however many times you cleaned her. Mum used to go to the market, Ridley Road market, while all this was going on.

After I'd cleaned the lavatory and scrubbed the passage right through and cleaned inside and outside of the windows (which wasn't very many, as we only had three rooms), my next job was to go and get our Saturday dinner, which was our favourite. A tuppeny and a pen'orth each – a tuppeny piece of fish (which you would now pay five bob for) and a pen'orth of chips (which would easy cost two bob today). And there were no plates to wash because we ate 'em out of a newspaper. It was absolutely lovely – we thoroughly enjoyed it. Jackie would come home from the pictures, tell us how Pearl White had got on and if she was still hanging over the cliff or if she was tied on to the rails.

After dinner all was quiet for a little while. Mum used to have a lie down with Dad. One of us would have to take Jimmy out in the pram, so that he wouldn't cry. Then my Dad would decide to get up. I must tell you here that his boots, that he always wore on a Saturday, were at the pawnshop. So Jackie, who was the fastest runner of all, used to get them. Dad didn't know where his boots were. While Dad was in the lavatory Jackie had to run like hell down to Grout's with the pawn ticket and the shilling to get Dad's boots out before Dad came out. He was always a long while in there – I don't know what he did because there was nothing in there, no windows. He might have been studying form, with the bum paper. I don't know. But whatever it was, he was always a long while, which was greatly to Mum's relief. She was the one that pawned the boots. Why he wore 'em on Saturday I don't know, but he did.

Why Dad always worked at night was that it was easier to rook a half-drunk toff at night coming out of the night clubs than it was to rook somebody in the daytime that just wanted a station job done. And my Dad was all for rooking. He would swear at night that a toff had given him a ten bob note when in reality they'd given him a pound. And then, being as they were, they'd say 'O.K. Driver' and give him a tip on top of that. Off Pa would go, as happy as the birds in spring. Being 17½ stone helped him there I expect.

Saturday night was bath night, which I hated, not because I hated a bath, but I hated the way it had to be done. It was such a small kitchen that the bath was kept hanging up on a nail out in the yard – a tin bath. It was such a small kitchen that it wouldn't go on the floor between the fireplace and the table. So it had to go *on* the table. Next door's kitchen overlooked our kitchen and they could see us all having our baths, which I did not like. We started from the youngest, leaving Jimmy out, 'cos he was a baby. We started with Phyllis, who was the luckiest of all, because she had clean water and the only two clean towels we had. Mum used to have big iron saucepans on top of the hob getting hotter all the time. My job was to dry the kids as they came out. We went in numbers, Phyllis first. It was very hard to dry Phyllis as she was partially paralysed and used to have a very bad temper. We had no nighties or pyjamas. We put our clean vest on and went and sat on the bed in the back room, because this was the night when we had a cup of cocoa, the only night of the week. Next came Jackie, who was always as black as your hat. The water is now getting slightly discoloured. Another saucepan of water goes in – hot water – and the towels are getting a bit damp. I dry Jackie and so on, till it gets to Charlie, who's 11. By this time, the towels are soaking wet. So Charlie has to dry himself on the other's dirty underclothes.

Last comes me. I kick up a stink because I don't want to stand on the table because the Wrights next door can see me. I get a wallop on my bare behind for a start. Another saucepan of water goes in and I get in to a pale grey soup. I have to wash my hair in this, which is very long. We all had to wash our hair in this. Eventually I have two wet towels, everybody's wet underclothes and my own dry underclothes to dry on.

Then came the performance of emptying the bath. We all had to get hold of an end here – Mum got hold of one end, because she was as strong as a lion. You notice I call her Mum. I've always called her Mum. She's still alive today – she's 85. And I always call the other kids sisters and brothers, although they are not, in reality. Mum got hold of one end of the bath, Charlie and I got hold of the other end and we used to scramble out, in our vests, to the backyard to empty the water down the drain and hang it up again on the wall out in the yard. Then we came in and we're all sitting in our vests, very dignified I must say. We have a cup of Perkses cocoa. Now

this was three ha'pence a quarter, and to us kids it was marvellous, 'cos we had condensed milk in it. It was the only night in the week that we had cocoa.

After such a hilarious day, Mum used to have her well-deserved Guinness, which by the way was not paid for – I had to go over previously to the Off Licence to have it put on the slate till next week, because Mum was not a good manager, as you can guess by Dad's boots being pawned. Then we all went to bed in the same way as we got out: Phyllis by the wall up the top, Jackie at the bottom with his feet in Phyllis' mouth, Winnie up the top, Charlie coming next, with his feet in Winnie's mouth, and me being the eldest, I was up the top on the end. I spent more time falling out of bed in those days than I've done in the whole of my life put together! Thus ended the happiest day of our lives – Saturday in 1920.

Lil Smith

Spare cash

Spare cash is the money you have left over after you have bought all the necessities. This chart shows how much was spent on leisure activities during 1982.

	Gross normal weekly income of household					
	Under £60	£60 and under £120	£120 and under £180	£180 and under £240	£240 or more	All households
Average weekly household expenditure (£s) on:						
Alcoholic drink	1.46	3.06	5.75	7.73	11.15	6.13
Books, newspapers, magazines, etc.	1.04	1.59	2.05	2.43	3.23	2.14
Television, radio, and musical instruments	1.34	2.01	3.06	4.56	6.05	3.55
Purchase of materials for home repairs, etc.	0.29	0.86	1.65	3.11	3.51	1.97
Holidays	0.41	1.12	2.57	3.17	10.62	3.99
Hobbies	0.01	0.04	0.07	0.13	0.15	0.08
Cinema admissions	0.02	0.05	0.08	0.10	0.21	0.10
Dance admissions	0.02	0.06	0.08	0.13	0.25	0.12
Theatre, concert, etc., admissions	0.03	0.05	0.12	0.15	0.44	0.18
Subscriptions and admission charges to participant sports	0.03	0.12	0.35	0.54	0.89	0.41
Football match admissions	–	0.01	0.08	0.07	0.10	0.06
Admissions to other spectator sports	–	–	0.02	0.02	0.05	0.02
Sports goods (excluding clothes)	0.01	0.07	0.18	0.53	0.40	0.24
Other entertainment	0.04	0.10	0.23	0.31	0.51	0.25
Total weekly expenditure on above	4.69	9.13	16.30	22.99	37.56	19.23
Expenditure on above items as a percentage of total household expenditure	9.4	10.6	13.3	14.7	16.7	14.4

Her Majesty's Stationery Office

Penny's home

Christopher Porter has a damaged leg. He has been befriended by the class outcast, Penny Marshall.

The steps were worn and slippery. Christopher got down them, plus the loaded carton, by sliding his hip against the wall. 'Never try and carry anything down stairs,' his mother warned him. 'What's a bump and a sprain to an ordinary boy could be three months in hospital to you,' his father often said. He had always listened to his mother, and to his father too. But had they been right? Here he was at the bottom of Penny's steps without disaster. What else might he manage to do, if he really tried? Look at Mister O'Brien, charging about on his crutches from the hospital to the school to Fishpond Street.

Penny produced from her coat pocket a large key tied to a length of electric flex. She shoved the key into a wooden door with MARSHALL painted on it in what looked like tomato sauce. Christopher was standing six feet below the level of the street. The stone slabs under him were slimy and green. Rain was dribbling down the steps. His arms were in a state of near collapse.

Penny charged the door with her shoulder. It burst open. 'Come in,' she said, as if inviting him into a place as respectable as his own. She stepped through the dark doorway and Christopher followed her.

That smell! It was Penny's smell, only fifty times worse. It reminded Christopher of toadstools and goldfish bowls that haven't been cleaned out and milk bottles full of fungus. He wanted to turn round and escape. But how could he? He couldn't hurt Penny's feelings when she'd been so nice, almost like a friend. Besides, he wouldn't want Mister O'Brien to see him running away.

'Who were you talking to?' Penny asked. She clicked a light on.

All his life Christopher Porter had lived in warm, bright rooms with carpets and curtains and pretty wallpaper, with electric fires and a television and a sofa and a washing machine and a vacuum cleaner, with white-painted ceilings and glossy paintwork and fruit in bowls and a fridge. Everything orderly and organized, the milk in a milk jug and the butter on a butter dish and the bread on a bread board, and the cups on saucers and the saucers on a tablecloth embroidered with flowers or birds. He lived like that and so did Tony Anderson and so did the children of his mother's friends on the committee of the Royal Society for the Prevention of Cruelty to Animals, and so did the other children in the road and the children of his father's colleagues in the local department of taxation. He knew no children who lived differently. He had seen poor homes, in the newspaper and occasionally on television, but these children hadn't seemed like real children but like acting children made up to look dirty, thin and sore. He had never really and truly, deep down inside him, believed that any family lived in a damp mouldy smelly cellar.

But this was what Penny Marshall's family did live in. A damp mouldy smelly cellar.

The first thing that hit Christopher between the eyebrows wasn't the newspaper tablecloth or the milk tins on the table or the margarine packets littered about. It wasn't the baby's nappies draped on a rope or the orange boxes that served as chairs or the naked light bulb or the tin bucket full of soggy grey clothes. What knocked him back were the walls. At first glance he thought they must be covered with a green and black wallpaper but when he looked longer he saw that the green was mould and the black was damp, with here and there a grey squiggle where plaster had freshly fallen off.

'Soon have a cup of tea going,' Penny said cheerfully.

She lit the gas stove with a flourish and filled a tin kettle from a tap low down in the wall, over what looked like a cattle trough. She didn't say, 'Sorry everything's in a mess.' Instead she said, 'Do sit down,' as if it were an easy chair and not an orange box she was offering him.

Christopher sat down and brought his feet together. Except that his bad leg didn't come. For a second he was puzzled. Then he realized that, for the first time that he could remember, he'd forgotten he had a bad leg. He had been so agog at the state of the place Penny lived in that he had forgotten that his bad leg didn't come of its own accord but had to be heaved.

The tea, in a chipped enamel mug, was the colour of conkers and thick with sugar. Christopher loved it. As he sipped it he wondered where Penny's father and mother and brothers and sisters were. He watched Penny slapping margarine on the sliced bread, tipping the beans into a saucepan and peeling potatoes in a bowl that she brought to the table. Every now and then she jumped up to feel the nappies over the gas stove. A girl of eleven doing all these housewife things? Christopher didn't even make his own bed. Where was Mrs Marshall? And where did everyone sleep?

Prudence Andrew

Horrible things

'What's the horriblest thing you've seen?'
Said Nell to Jean.

'Some grey-coloured, trodden-on plasticine;
On a plate, a left-over cold baked bean;
A cloak-room ticket numbered thirteen;
A slice of meat without any lean;
The smile of a spiteful fairy-tale queen;
A thing in the sea like a brown submarine;
A cheese fur-coated in brilliant green;
A bluebottle perched on a piece of sardine.
What's the horriblest thing *you've* seen?'
Said Jean to Nell.

'Your face, as you tell
Of all the horriblest things you've seen.'

Roy Fuller

A removal from Terry Street

On a squeaking cart, they push the usual stuff,
A mattress, bed ends, cups, carpets, chairs,
Four paperback westerns. Two whistling youths
In surplus U.S. Army battle-jackets
Remove their sister's goods. Her husband
Follows, carrying on his shoulders the son
Whose mischief we are glad to see removed,
And pushing, of all things, a lawnmower.
There is no grass in Terry Street. The worms
Come up cracks in concrete yards in moonlight.
That man, I wish him well. I wish him grass.

Douglas Dunn

Market day in Jamaica

'The sun rose lazily from behind Blue Mountain. A cock
crowed loudly in the yard next door. The air was fresh and
clean and the grass sparkled with early morning dew. In the
distance, voices could be heard, some of excitement and
some of just plain boredom. Yes, it was here. Market day had
arrived.'

On the way to the market, both women and men can be seen
balancing loads on their heads. The women having straw
baskets filled with yams, cacao, fruit of all kinds, drinking
chocolate, peas and beans. You name it and they have it. I
usually wondered what would happen if the baskets should
fall off. The men have similar loads, some containing hand-
made cups, mugs, plates, cutlery, wooden bowls and dishes,
straw hats, sandals, lots of things I can't name. A song will
suddenly burst into tune, 'Carry me ackee go ah Linstead
markit, not a quatly woth sell.' All are going to the market for
the same reason, though, to catch the eyes of the tourists
who come in by boat to the town harbour.

A voice is heard shouting, 'Sa-vanna-la-mar markit!' At this,
everyone piles out of the bus. It is like a stampede with
everyone rushing to the stalls, trying to get the best goods
first. I make my way with great difficulty through the crowd
and stop to talk to Daisy, a vendor. She has problems as
usual. 'Listen 'ere, girl chil', yuh know seh de dutty man
Godfrey gone lef' me wid de ten pickney.' I shake my head in
pity. But she doesn't give me a chance to express this before
she's off again, 'Dat's why ah always tell yuh to stay away from
man. Dem is a dirty set.' A woman comes to the stall and I take
this chance to slip away. As I walk off, I hear her shouting,
'Look 'ere 'oman, if yuh not buying nuthin' don't feel up me
things. Dat's all unu come 'ere fi do.' I do not hear the rest.

The other stalls are basically the same, some having the same
merchandise as the others. There is always something
interesting to see in the crowds; dudes on the piazzas eyeing
the chicks, hustlers trying to sell their make-believe jewellery
and one or two pickpockets. After the stalls, there are women,
children or men selling food. One lady in particular is
shouting, 'Yam, cocoa, green banana, bammies, anything yuh
want, come 'ere so an' get it.' A vendor and a woman are
arguing about the price of an avocado pear. The woman says,
'Dis yah dry up fluxy pear yuh want me fi pay 70 cents fa? Yuh
can keep i', ah wouldn' gi it to me dawg if 'im was arf dead fi
'ungry.'

The vendors says, 'Lady, don' bring yuh freshness to mi, if yuh
think i' fluxy move on. Somebody ah go buy i' any way. Is not
you one mi 'ave fi custama.'

Passing the food section, we arrive at the butcher's and
fishmonger's section. The butcher is a fat, swarthy man
covered with big black moles. He looks like a polka-dot cow or
manged brown dog. Despite his appearance, he is quite a
friendly fellow. 'Ello missie,' says he to me, 'a've got di t-bone
steak yuh wanted. Picked it specially fi yuh.' He asks me about
my parents for a while and we have a little chat before I move
on. A fishmonger shouts, 'Feeesh! Sprat! Jack! Butter! Yuh
name i' and mi got i'! Feeesh!' There is nothing else after this,
really. Just a few stalls with one or two things. I turn and go
into a cafe, order a large, long glass of iced cold lemonade
and sit back and watch what-seems-like-the-whole-world go by.

Suzanne Chantal Neita

I'm the big sleeper

I'm the big sleeper
rolled up in his sheets
at the break of day

I'm a big sleeper living soft
in a hard kind of way

The light through the curtain
can't wake me
I'm under the blankets

you can't shake me
the pillow rustler
and the blanket gambler
a mean tough eiderdown man

I keep my head
I stay in bed.

Michael Rosen

The fight of the year

'And there goes the bell for the third month
and Winter comes out of its corner looking groggy
Spring leads with a left to the head
followed by a sharp right to the body
    daffodils
    primroses
    crocuses
    snowdrops
    lilacs
    violets
    pussywillow

Winter can't take much more punishment
and Spring shows no signs of tiring
    tadpoles
    squirrels
    baalambs
    badgers
    bunny rabbits
    mad march hares
    horses and hounds
Spring is merciless

Winter won't go the full twelve rounds
    bobtail clouds
    scallywaggy winds
    the sun
    a pavement artist
    in every town
A left the the chin
and Winter's down!
    1 tomatoes
    2 radish
    3 cucumber
    4 onions
    5 beetroot
    6 celery
    7 and any
    8 amount
    9 of lettuce
    10 for dinner
Winter's out for the count
Spring is the winner!'

Roger McGough

Ice on the Round Pond

This was a dog's day, when the land
Lay black and white as a Dalmatian
And kite chased terrier kite
In a Kerry Blue sky.

This was a boy's day, when the wind
Cuts tracks in the sky on skates
And noon leaned over like a snowman
To melt in the sun.

This was a poet's day, when the mind
Lay paper-white in a winter's peace
And watched the printed bird-tracks
Turn into words.

Paul Dehn

ACKNOWLEDGEMENTS

We wish to thank all those authors and publishers who have given permission to reproduce copyright material in this anthology. Writing previously published elsewhere is included by kind permission of the publishers whose names appear first after each entry in the Index. All material first published in this anthology is copyright © 1985 Mary Glasgow Publications Ltd.

We are grateful to the following for permission to reproduce photographs: Sally and Richard Greenhill, pages 4 and 38 (bottom); Carlos Reyes/Andes Press Agency, pages 5 (top), 36, 37 and 74; The Photo Source/Keystone, pages 5 (bottom) and 33; Fay Godwin's Photo Files, pages 7 and 20; BBC Hulton Picture Library, pages 10-11 and 85; Manchester Studies Department, Manchester Polytechnic, pages 13 (donated to the archives by Mrs Annie Atkin) and 38 (top) (donated by Helen Watt); the NSPCC, pages 26-7; Frank Lane Agency, pages 44, 47, 50-1 and 52; David Dore, page 46; Peta Hambling, page 60; Polytrantic Press, page 61; Thames Television, page 73; The Deighton Consultancy, page 75; Rex Features, page 80; Dr G. I. Jones, page 81; Mary Evans Picture Library, page 90, and Anne Bolt, page 93.

The illustrations on pages 45 and 57 are by Anni Axworthy; on pages 55, 83 and 94 by Ann Baum; on pages 58-9, 76 and 89 by Harry Constantine; on pages 16 and 30 by Jane Cope; on pages 48-9 and 50 by Sian Davies; on pages 2, 17, 42 and 88 by Graham Higgins; on pages 14, 63 and 78 by David Parkins; on page 8 by Trevor Parkin; on page 23 by Gary Rees; on pages 9, 28 and 69 by Martin Salisbury, and on pages 18-19, 65 and 71 by Barrie Thorpe.

INDEX

(Advertisement): TBWA *for the Department of Health and Social Security*, reproduced with the permission of the Controller, Her Majesty's Stationery Office, **35**

Aiken, Joan: 'Mortimer', from *The bread bin*, BBC Publications Ltd, **58**

Allum, Marie: 'The wrong doing', first published in this anthology, **21**

Andrew, Prudence: 'Penny's home', from *Mister O'Brien*, William Heinemann Ltd, **92**

Andrews, Julie: 'That's me', from *My world*, ed. J. Griffiths, BBC Publications Ltd, **33**

(Anon.): 'Happy Christmas', first published in this anthology, **83**

(Anon.): 'Heathcliffe', from *Finding the words: Cumbria pupils' writing*, Cumbria Education Committee, **45**

Archer, Kim: 'Buying a pet', from *Reflections: a Suffolk schools anthology*, Suffolk Education Authority, **60**

Armour, Richard: 'Copy', from *Being born and growing older*, ed. B. Vance, William Heinemann Ltd, **1**

Ashley, Bernard: 'Billy's game', from *All my men*, Oxford University Press, paperback by Puffin Books, **68**

Ashley, Bernard: 'Terry', from *Terry on the fence*, Oxford University Press, paperback by Puffin Books, **29**

Avery, Valerie: 'No good crying now', from *London spring*, William Kimber and Co. Ltd, **10**

Batchelor, Joan M: 'The cover', from *Home truths: Writings by North West women*, Commonword Writers' Workshop, **77**

Batchelor, Joan M: 'My birthday treat', from *On the wild side*, Commonword Writers' Workshop, **14**

Batchelor, Joan M: 'Next best thing', from *On the wild side*, Commonword Writers' Workshop, **6**

de Beauvoir, Simone: 'Family album', from *Memoirs of a dutiful daughter* (English translation by J. Kirkup), Andre Deutsch Ltd/ Weidenfeld and Nicolson Ltd, paperback by Penguin Books, **4**

Blume, Judy: 'I don't think I'll ever get married', from *It's not the end of the world*, William Heinemann Ltd, paperback by Pan Books, **22**

Blume, Judy: 'That dumb old dog', from *Otherwise known as Sheila the Great*, The Bodley Head, paperback by Pan Books (Piccolo), **54**

Bosley, Keith: 'Ferret', from *A fourth poetry book*, ed. J. Foster, Oxford University Press, **50**

Boundy, Susan: 'My gran', from *The English Programme Poetry Competition 1982 winners and runners up*, Thames Television International Ltd, **37**

Boyton, Denise: 'Zeeta', first published in this anthology, **46**

Brindley, Christian: 'The newspaper lady', first published in this anthology, **9**

Byars, Betsy: 'Nobody's putting me in no garbage can', from *The eighteenth emergency*, The Bodley Head, paperback by Puffin Books, **62**

Byars, Betsy: 'Unexpected charge of an enraged bull', from *The eighteenth emergency*, The Bodley Head, paperback by Puffin Books, **57**

Clarke, Lucy: 'The Lindens', first published in this anthology, **39**

Clayton, Tracey: 'The turtles', from *A4*, Schools' Poetry Association, **52**

Clegg, Susan: 'Watch this', first published in this anthology, **6**

Dehn, Paul: 'Ice on the Round Pond', from *The fern on the rock*, Hamish Hamilton Ltd; also in *All day long*, ed. P. Whitlock, Oxford University Press, **94**

Dunn, Douglas: 'A removal from Terry Street', from *Terry Street*, Faber and Faber Ltd, **92**

Firth, L, ed: 'Keeping small mammals', from *Have fun with nature, book 4*, Macdonald and Co. Ltd, **44**

Freedman, Daniel: 'Freedman', first published in this anthology, **15**

Fuller, Roy: 'Horrible things', from *Seen grandpa lately?*, Andre Deutsch Ltd, **92**

Gibson, Douglas: 'White cat in moonlight', from *Happy landings*, Evans Brothers Ltd, **48**

Gilbert, John: 'I'm the hard one!', first published in this anthology, **61**

Gowar, Mick: 'Dinner party blues', from *Swings and roundabouts*, William Collins and Sons Ltd, **88**

Graham, Paul: 'Grandfather and I', first published in this anthology, **36**

Grant, Gwen: 'Too much water', from *Knock and wait*, William Heinemann Ltd, paperback by Armada Books, **67**

Greene, Bette: extract from *Philip Hall likes me. I reckon maybe.*, Hamish Hamilton Ltd, paperback by Puffin Books, **64**

Grieves, Thomas: 'Why?', first published in this anthology, **16**

Guy, Rosa: 'Edith', from *The friends*, Victor Gollancz Ltd, paperback by Puffin Books, **72**

Hardman, Ian: 'Round one', first published in this anthology, **61**

Harris, Roderick: 'The hand', first published in this anthology, **75**

Her Majesty's Stationery Office: 'Spare cash', from *Social Trends 1982*, **91**

Hines, Barry: 'Tadpoles', from *A Kestrel for a Knave*, Michael Joseph Ltd, paperback *Kes* by Penguin Books, **14**

Hinsley, Clarissa: 'My newts', from *Moving jewels: an anthology of pupils' writing*, Cambridgeshire Local Education Authority, **51**

Hrynkow, Susan: 'Grandfather', from *Young people's poetry*, North West Arts, **36**

Jackson, Alan: 'Goldfish', from *Strictly private*, ed. Roger McGough, Penguin Books (Puffin Plus), **60**

James, Sammy: 'What a brother!', first published in this anthology, **28**

James, Susanne: 'Dad', first published in this anthology, **18**

Joannou, Angela: 'Wedding bells: Greek style', from *A wonderful dream*, ed. A. Aston, Inner London Education Authority, **80**

Kathleen _____ : 'Tears', from *Enjoying writing*, ed. A. Clegg, Chatto and Windus Ltd, **1**

Keenan, Kevin: 'The lion', from *Seize on life*, Cumbria Education Committee, **52**

Larkin, Philip: 'Take one home for the kiddies', from *The Whitsun weddings*, Faber and Faber Ltd, **47**

Leather, Brenda: 'Tara Mam', from *Home truths: writings by North-West women*, Commonword Writers' Workshop, **8**

Lenzi, Martina: 'Saved from silence', first published in this anthology, **3**

Lucie-Smith, Edward: 'The lesson', from *Modern poetry*, ed. J. R. Townsend, Oxford University Press, **18**

McGough, Roger: 'The fight of the year', from *Watchwords*, Jonathan Cape Ltd, **94**

Mark, Jan: 'I'll tell your mum', from *The short voyage of the Albert Ross*, Granada Publishing Ltd, **74**

Mark, Jan: 'William's version', from *Nothing to be afraid of*, Penguin Books (Puffin), **40**

Marquis, Don: 'Tom-cat', from *Archy and Mehitabel*, Faber and Faber Ltd, **49**

Marsh, C: 'Nothing', first published in this anthology, **47**

Marshall, Lorna: 'At Strachur', first published in this anthology, **7**

Masters, Christopher: 'Power drill', first published in this anthology, **21**

Moody, Helen: 'The row', from *Broadsheet poems 8*, Schools' Poetry Association, **20**

Moody, Helen: 'Skeleton!', from A4, Schools' Poetry Association, **60**

Needle, Jan: 'Signed: Your friend', from *My mate Shofiq*, Andre Deutsch Ltd and Fontana Paperbacks, **71**

Neita, Suzanne Chantal: 'Market day in Jamaica', from *A wonderful dream*, ed. A. Aston, Inner London Education Authority, **93**

Notley High School pupils: 'Our dads', first published in this anthology, **16**

Nilsson, Lennart: 'As small as the point of a pin', from *How you began*, Penguin Books (Kestrel), **1**

NSPCC: extract from Annual Review and Annual Report, 1982, **25**

Nzekwu, Onuora: 'The funeral dance', from *Wand of noble wood*, Hutchinson Publishing Group Ltd; also in *African writing – a thematic anthology*, ed. P. Zabala and C. Rossell, Collins Educational, **81**

O'Connor, Frank: 'The genius', from *Stories of Frank O'Connor: My Oedipus complex and other stories*, Hamish Hamilton Ltd, **2**

O'Sullivan, Sharon: 'November 5th', first published in this anthology, **83**

Owen, Gareth: 'Photograph', from *Salford Road*, Penguin Books (Kestrel), **5**

Owen, Gareth: 'Salford Road', from *Salford Road*, Penguin Books (Kestrel), **13**

Patten, Brian: 'A small dragon', from *Notes from a hurrying man*, George Allen and Unwin Ltd; also in *My world*, ed. J. Griffiths, BBC Publications Ltd, **52**

Pearce, Philippa: 'Rats!', from *The battle of Bubble and Squeak*, Andre Deutsch Ltd, paperback by Puffin Books, **43**

Ray, Marion: 'Indian childhood', first published in this anthology, **8**

Robinson, Barbara: 'The worst kids in the world', from *The best Christmas Pageant ever*, Faber and Faber Ltd, paperback by Beaver Books (title: *The worst kids in the world*), **76**

Roethke, Theodore: 'My papa's waltz' from *The collected poems of Theodore Roethke*, Hearst Magazines/University of Washington Press, USA, **48**

Rosen, Michael: 'I'm the big sleeper', from *Mind your own business*, Andre Deutsch Ltd, paperback by Armada Books, **94**

Rosen, Michael: 'Look', from *Wouldn't you like to know*, Andre Deutsch Ltd, paperback by Puffin Books, **89**

Rowe, Linda: 'Anger', from 'The anger was all over my legs . . . in *Fire words*, ed. C. Searle, Jonathan Cape Ltd, **76**

Ryba, Audrey: 'The culprit of the vase', first published in this anthology, **24**

Seabrook, Jeremy: 'Jealousy', from *Working-class childhood*, Victor Gollancz Ltd, **32**

Shepherd, Chris E: 'Angela', first published in this anthology, **32**

Shyer, Marlene Fanta: 'Firecracker', from *Welcome home, Jellybean*, Granada Publishing Ltd, (Dragon paperback), **34**

Simpson, Matt: 'Bonfire Night and Mr Ellison', from *Making arrangements*, Bloodaxe Books Ltd, **82**

Skeldon, Karen: 'The weekly experience', from *Anvil*, ed. Dr W. Cooke, Stoke-on-Trent Sixth Form College, **89**

Smith, Lil: 'Any Saturday in 1920', from *Working lives 1*, Centerprise Trust Ltd, **89**

Smith, Steven: 'My sister', first published in this anthology, **28**

Springer, Susan: 'Yes, I can remember the coal mines', from *Reflections: a Suffolk schools anthology*, Suffolk Education Authority, **37**

Stuart, Derek: 'My gramp', from *A second poetry book*, ed. J. L. Foster, Oxford University Press, **37**

Teitelbaum, Julie: 'Alice Dear', from *Uptaught*, ed. K. Macrorie, Hayden Book Co. Inc., New Jersey, USA, **13**

Tessimond, A. S. J: 'Cats', from *All day long*, ed. P. Whitlock, Oxford University Press, reproduced by permission of the author's executor, **48**

Thomas, Leslie: 'Breadcrumb's birthday', from *This time next week*, Constable Publishers, paperback by Pan Books, **87**

Thomas, Leslie: 'Monkey', from *This time next week*, Constable Publishers, paperback by Pan Books, **70**

Vassili, Demetroulla: 'Don't interrupt', from *City lines*, The English Centre, Inner London Education Authority, **20**

Walker, Margaret: 'Lineage', from *For my people*, Yale University Press, USA; also in *The Penguin book of women poets*, ed. C. Cosman (paperback), **36**

Walsh, John: 'How to catch newts', from 'My world', ed. J. Griffiths, BBC Publications Ltd, © Mrs A. M. Walsh, **50**

Waterhouse, Keith: 'Albert and the liner', from *Dandelion clocks*, ed. A. Bradley and K. Jamieson, Michael Joseph Ltd, paperback by Penguin Books, **84**

Weisbloom, Harry: 'The Cruelty man', *The Listener*, 11 November 1982, **26**

Wells, Colin: 'Going, going, it's here again', first published in this anthology, **18**

Whillans, Don: 'My world', from *Portrait of a mountaineer* (by Don Whillans and Alick Ormerod), William Heinemann Ltd, **7**

White, C: 'Looking back', first published in this anthology, **5**

Williams, David: 'Right!', first published in this anthology, **62**

Wright, Kit: 'The budgie's New Year message', from *Hot dog and other poems*, Penguin Books Ltd (Kestrel), **88**

Wright, Kit: 'Me and my family', from *Rabbiting on*, Fontana Paperbacks, **42**

Woman from Southampton: see Seabrook, Jeremy

Wright, Kit: 'My dad, your dad', from *Rabbiting on*, Fontana Paperbacks, **17**